WESTWARD THE NATION IN SONG, DANCE AND STORY

Lena Stuart Minugh

and

Nancy Keochakian Cory

Lancaster School District
Lancaster, California

Cover

William Schiffmacher

Illustrations

John Arensma   Richard W. Draney
Ronald E. Crooks   John A. Solie
Jan M. Domela   Noël Quinn

CALIFORNIA STATE SERIES
Published by
CALIFORNIA STATE DEPARTMENT OF EDUCATION
Sacramento, 1967

ACKNOWLEDGMENTS

Appreciation is expressed to the following California educators who evaluated sections of the original manuscript of WESTWARD THE NATION IN SONG, DANCE AND STORY:

Patricia Dobson, Consultant in Education, Sunnyvale Elementary School District;

Landon A. Dunn, Consultant in Elementary Education, Solano County Schools, Fairfield;

Lucille Gansberg, Consultant in Education, Sacramento County Schools;

Elizabeth C. Kay, Supervisor of Elementary Education, Chula Vista Elementary School District;

Richard Rutherford, Elementary Administrator, Bakersfield Elementary School District; and

Mildred Simmons, Consultant in Elementary Education, Riverside Unified School District.

Special recognition is extended to Jane N. Wilson, San Diego, who adapted the music for the text, and to Ruth L. Roche, Professor of Education, San Fernando Valley State College, Northridge, who worked as educational consultant to the authors throughout the development of this project.

CONTENTS

FOOTPRINTS

If you would know a people's story, travel the people's roads.
The history in the books is a tale that men set down in words of their own making.
But the roads are their footsteps, the paths of their restless dreams.
Deep in the dust are the prints of their feet,
Questing feet, restless feet with the urge of travel upon them,
Hurrying feet eager to get there first,
Weary feet trudging under heavy loads.

Winding roads in the hill country where jolting wagons followed the flow of water and men
   trudged beside them into the wilderness.
The curving roads of the prairies, skirting the fields, fitting themselves to the farmer and his
   needs.
Mountain roads, seeking the notch and the pass, where the traveler might cross over into the
   new land.
The roads of the plains, like an arrow's flight.
Desert roads, from water to water.

—Hal. G. Borland

"Footprints" from *America to Americans*. Published by Harper and Brothers, copyright 1941 by Hal G. Borland.

CHAPTER I

WEST TO THE MISSISSIPPI

Traveling Along on the Western Roads

As you think about the early Americans who found the courage to move westward into an unknown land, ask yourself, "What if I had lived then? What would it have been like to have traveled west with the pioneers?"

In this book you will travel the wilderness trails to find out how these early settlers lived, worked, played—and met the everyday dangers around them. Pictures in the book will show you the ingenious things they made. With no factories on the frontier, and with few trading posts, nearly *everything* had to be made by hand.

Children had an important part in frontier life. They worked side by side with their parents at nearly all the pioneer tasks. But they had fun, too. They played as hard as they worked. They even made up many of their own games, dances and songs.

As you move west with them in this book, you may discover that you sing some of the same songs and read some of the same folk tales that were told so long ago in settlers' cabins and around campfires. You may find that you do some of the same dances and play some of the same games.

When you were younger, maybe you even said this jump-rope rhyme that your great-great-grandparents knew:

Johnny over the ocean,
Johnny over the sea,
Johnny broke a teacup
And blamed it on me.
I told ma.
Ma told Pa.
Johnny got a lickin'.
Hah, hah, hah!
Salt, vinegar,
Mustard, PEPPER!

Pioneer children began to count fast after the word "pepper." They counted faster and faster to test the ability of the jumper. Is this the way you did it, too?

Everyone Wanted To Go West

Our young country was feeling very proud after the Revolutionary War, and particularly so after the War of 1812. We had defeated the greatest empire in the world, and we were ready for new adventures. There was this big, mysterious country west of our Appalachian Mountains. We wondered what was there.

Some people struggled over the mountains just to find out. Farmers went because they heard that the land grew better crops. Many of the pioneers were immigrants from the troubled countries of the world, and they were looking for free land and a freer life.

The people who went first had to follow wild animal paths and Indian trails. Those who were not killed by Indians, by wild animals, by bad weather or by accidents along the wilderness trails, came back from the valleys of the Ohio with stories about a land of great forests and beautiful meadows, of clear lakes and wide rivers —a land filled with deer and buffalo, birds and fish. Travelers said that there was food enough for everybody, plenty of furs for clothing and for trading, free land ready for the plow, and rich ores and minerals close under the ground.

Excited by these stories, people packed their household goods on the backs of horses or mules—or on their own backs—picked up their rifles and went west. And none were so poor but what they carried in their minds and hearts many songs, dances and stories that had come to America from other lands.

As we move west with the pioneers, let's begin with finding out about life on the first trails, crude roads and turnpikes. Over these paths people traveled on foot, on horseback, and later in wagons and stagecoaches. Before trails were made wide enough for wheeled vehicles, people moved most of their possessions on pack-horses.

What experiences do you think pioneer people had as they moved along this trail to a new land? Do you think they sang as they traveled along? What might they do as they sat around their wilderness fires at night? Do you think the children grew tired? Did they have a chance to play?

The Wilderness Trail

Bureau of Public Roads

The Wilderness Road and Daniel Boone

As a young boy, Daniel Boone listened to tales about the wonderful Kentucky country beyond the Allegheny Mountains. He heard it described as a hunter's paradise, a place where buffalo were so big that the meadows sank down under their weight, and where there were so many wild turkeys it was impossible for all of them to fly at the same time.

Daniel Boone determined to find a way into this wilderness wonderland, and he did. He blazed the Wilderness Road through the Cumberland Gap and opened up the country to settlers.

Folktales about this frontier hunter and Indian fighter have made him one of America's favorite heroes. Folktales are stories circulated among a people by word-of-mouth. In pioneer days there were no television programs or movies, of course. There were not even very many books. During long winter evenings some kind of amusement was necessary, and story-telling became an art.

These folktales of the American frontier were of all kinds. Some were filled with wonder and enchantment; some were about animals that talked. There were trickster stories, tall tales, riddles, frightening stories, and legends of heroes and strong men. Many stories were told about imaginary folk-heroes, but some folk-heroes actually lived. Daniel Boone was such a hero. People thought of him as strong, wise, cunning and brave.

Did you ever hear the story of how Daniel Boone met his wife? As a part of this story you will read about a way of hunting animals that is illegal today. It would be punished by a heavy fine because it does not give animals a chance for their lives. But on the frontier where there were no stockyards nor meat markets, men had to hunt animals for food. They also had to devise ways of getting close enough to shoot without wasting gunpowder. Why was it important to save gunpowder?

How Daniel Boone Met His Wife

One dark night Daniel Boone, with a young friend, was on a "fire hunt."

In a fire hunt, one hunter rode his horse ahead and carried what was called a "fire pan." The fire pan was full of blazing pine knots which sent a bright and flickering light far through the forest. The second hunter stayed a little behind, with his rifle ready for action.

A deer, lying quietly in his hidden bed, would be awakened by the approaching hunters. Instead of running, the deer usually remained frozen to the spot, staring into the light. The hunter could spot the deer when the light was reflected in its eyes. This cruel way of killing an animal was called "shining the eyes."

On this particular night, young Boone and his friend had followed a deer into thick timberland along a stream. The friend carried the fire pan; Boone carried the rifle. It was early in the evening, but the moon had not yet come up. Near Morgan Bryan's plantation, or farm, Boone's friend gave the usual signal to stop, meaning that he thought he had seen a deer.

Boone, after making certain that his rifle was in order, moved up very quietly behind a clump of bushes to get near enough for a sure shot. He could see the light reflected from two eyes. He put his rifle to his shoulder and sighted down the long barrel. It would be an easy shot; he couldn't miss.

But at the last instant he held his fire as a feeling of uneasiness trickled down his spine. Deep in the dark woods somewhere he heard an owl's sad hooting, and from the direction of Morgan Bryan's farm cabin a dog barked. There was certainly nothing about an owl hoot or a dog's bark to give a woodsman this uneasy feeling. There just wasn't any sense to it at all, Boone decided, and his finger started tightening again on the trigger to "make the shot."

But that instant's delay had given the creature in the woods a chance to move. It started running and Boone took after it, following the sound of woodland twigs and leaves crushed under foot. Once he raised his rifle to shoot at the sound but he lowered it again when he thought of the risk of wasting his lead and gunpowder. The creature running

from him was headed toward Morgan Bryan's hayfield, and Boone thought he might get a better shot there.

Boone was gaining, but when they reached the hayfield fence, the creature he was chasing cleared the rails with a leap. Boone, with his heavy rifle, had to stop and climb over the fence. The last he saw of it, his quarry was headed for the farm cabin. The dogs didn't bark, and Boone thought that was strange.

They did bark when *he* came stumbling close in the darkness. The cabin door opened and Boone could see the farmer in the doorway with the lamplight shining behind him.

As soon as Boone could catch his breath, he asked, "Have you got a pet deer, Mr. Bryan? I think maybe I flushed it in the woods. It ran straight for your cabin here."

"Yes," Mr. Bryan said, "I do have a pet dear." He started laughing as Boone came close. "You're Daniel Boone, aren't you? Come in . . . come in."

The first thing Boone saw when he entered the cabin was a young, blue-eyed girl panting for breath and looking frightened to death. Boone just stared at her, leaning weakly on his rifle, unable to say a word. He thought she was the prettiest girl he had ever seen. *And he had been trying to shoot her!*

The girl's father, Mr. Bryan, made the introductions. "Rebecca, this is young Daniel, son of our neighbor."

With Daniel it was "love at first sight." Rebecca's eyes had "shined his heart" as surely as a deer's eyes would have "shined" a bullet from his rifle. Rebecca must have felt somewhat the same way about it, because it wasn't long before she was happily married to her "terrible pursuer."

For some years then, Daniel Boone was kept busy hunting and farming in order to feed his growing family. But still he wanted to see Kentucky. He had heard about an Indian trail, the Warriors' Path, which led there. He persuaded his brother, Squire, his brother-in-law, John Stuart, and a few others to go. They set out in 1769.

Heading west from North Carolina, Boone found the trail he was seeking. Indians on the warpath had used it for centuries. After Boone blazed it and cleared away some of the rocks and tree roots, pioneers by the thousands followed the Warriors' Path through Cumberland Gap into Kentucky.

The poem, *The Tall Men*, tells something about the hardships and courage of these men as they searched for trails west. As you read the poem on the next page, think about the land over which Boone traveled. Locate this land on a map.

The Tall Men

Pack saddles, pack saddles, rocking through
 the passes,
Through the narrow mountain gaps,
 Cumberland and Pine,
Up the steep and shelving slope, round the
 boulder masses,
Down where under virgin woods flows
 Nepepermine!

Deer hunters, deer hunters, keen and greatly
 daring,
Following the bison track over root and bole,
Silent-footed, falcon-eyed, grave or gay in
 bearing,
Founders, builders, pressing on, knowing not
 their goal!

Down the Chatterawha, the Ohio and the
 Green,
The Cumberland, the Licking and the
 waterways between,
They found the trail they wanted or they
 made it with the axe—
The hunters of Kentucky with their rifles
 and their packs.
They built their lonely stations and the logs
 were cut and hewn
By the breed of Simon Kenton and the blood
 of Daniel Boone.
     —Arthur Guiterman

The westward migration over the Appalachians to a new kind of life lent itself to the creation of song. Men on expeditions and men in danger, men on lonely fron-tiers and men in dark forests sang. They sang for courage and for cheer. They sang because they were proud. Women who cared for their children in the wilderness sang their own lullabies and made up their own work songs. Singing was one of the chief forms of recreation on the frontier.

In those early pioneer days a family traveled afoot, carrying its household goods on a couple of pack horses, along with an axe and rifle. They could take little with them that reminded them of their old homes. In their memories, though, they carried beloved old tunes and ballads. Imagine a group of pioneers traveling along and singing the ballad *John Riley*. When you read the different verses, you can see that they tell the story of a man's journey back to England to get his bride.

John Riley

Smoothly

1. As I walked out one morn-ing ear-ly, To breathe the sweet and pleas-ant air, Who should I spy but a fair young maid-en, Whose cheeks were like the li-ly fair?

2 I stepped up to her and kindly asked her
If she would be a sailor's wife.
'O no, kind sir, I'd rather tarry
And remain single for all my life.'

3 'The truth, kind sir, I'll plainly tell you,
I could have married three years ago
To one John Riley who left this country,
Who has been the cause of my grief and woe.'

4 'Come along with me, don't think of Riley.
Come go with me to a distant shore.
We will set sail for Pennsylvany,
Adieu to England for evermore.'

5 'I'll not go with you to Pennsylvany,
I'll not go with you to a distant shore;
For my heart is with Riley and I can't forget him,
Although I may never see him no more.'

6 Now when he saw that she loved him truly,
He gave her kisses one, two, three,
Saying, 'I am Riley, your long-lost lover,
Who has been the cause of your misery.'

7 'If you be he and your name be Riley,
I will go with you to that distant shore,
We will set sail for Pennsylvany,
Adieu to England for evermore.'

"John Riley" by Alan Lomax, used by permission of Ludlow Music, Inc., New York.

Cumberland Gap was the gateway into the West for people from Virginia, Maryland, Delaware and the Carolinas. A high, bleak pass in the mountains, it looked as if it might have been chopped out of the solid rock with one, swift stroke of a giant axe. The Gap was the big "milestone" of the journey west, because after that the trail led downward in easier stages to the promised lands of Kentucky. When one reached the Gap, it was cause for a celebration.

Although the fiddle was the most common musical instrument in the saddlebags of the pioneers, even this was rare. However, many of these settlers were masters of the Celtic art of mouth music, the rhymed verses that matched the dance tunes and guided the feet of dancers back in Scotland. Americanized Scots continued to make rhymes in this way:

Buckskin moccasin, towheaded Bill
Once went a-courtin' up Jingleberry Hill,
The first one courted was a pretty gal to see,
They sat right down to Jingleberry tea.
Possum sop and polecat jelly
I ate so much I burst my belly.
Me and my gal and her granpap
All danced the jig in Cumberland Gap.

These so-called fiddle-songs were the favorite songs of Boone, and they were probably the first native pioneer songs. They helped in the taming of this new land, for when things were named and sung about, they became familiar and friendly.

Tax collectors, lawyers and preachers were left far behind over the mountains. In "Ol' Kaintuck," a man had elbow room. Here the "Kentucky screamers" who felt themselves to be "half-man, half-horse and half-alligator" behaved as they "bodaciously" pleased.

Look at the second line of the chorus in this song. Do you see that "Mmm" is starred (*)? What does this mean? As you sing, try to imagine that you are a "Kentucky screamer."

Cumberland Gap

Rowdy

1. Me an' my wife an' my wife's pap, We all live down in Cum-ber-land Gap.

CHORUS

Cum-ber-land Gap, Cum-ber-land Gap, _____

Mmm _____ * 'way down yon-der in Cum-ber-land Gap.

2 Cumberland Gap is a noted place,
  Three kinds of water to wash your face. (CHORUS)

3 The first white man in Cumberland Gap
  Was Doctor Walker, an English chap. (CHORUS)

4 Daniel Boone on Pinnacle Rock,
  He killed Injuns with his old flintlock. (CHORUS)

5 Lay down, boys, and take a little nap,
  Fo'teen miles to the Cumberland Gap. (CHORUS)

* *A hum that turns into a yell.*

Library of Congress

Turnpikes

The 1790's were known as the turnpike era in westward transportation. In 1795, the first toll road in the United States was built. This was the Lancaster Turnpike which connected Philadelphia and Lancaster in Pennsylvania. Every ten miles or so, long poles, tipped with sharp "pikes," or "spikes," were placed across the road to stop travelers. When a toll, or fee, was paid, the poles were turned out of the way to allow the travelers to proceed. As a result, such roads came to be called "turnpikes."

The turnpike era was something new in American inland travel. Before this, the roads were only wide enough for travelers on horseback, followed by packhorses. Cattle, hogs, sheep, ducks, turkeys and geese were driven along by animal herdsmen called "drovers." This song tells the story of a "hog drover" asking for a night's "largin", or lodging. As you read the words of the song, you will discover some that are strange and appear to be misspelled. You might like to learn this song.

Hog Drovers was popular as a "play-party" game on many frontiers. In certain areas, church rules forbade dancing to the music of a fiddle. Instead, some people played games at community parties to the rhythm of their own singing. Invitations to these play-parties, given by word of mouth, were often delivered by one or more young men on horseback. All of the young people for several miles around were invited. The "playing" started as soon as four or five couples arrived. Usually the party lasted until the early hours of the morning. The playing consisted of keeping step to the singing and at the same time going through various movements. Partners swung by one hand or both, advanced, retreated and bowed.

You may want to play this pioneer play-party game. You even might like to add your own verses and play the movements of the words.

Hog Drovers

With a swing

1. Hog drov - ers, hog drov - ers, hog drov - ers we air, A -
court - in' your daugh - ter, so hand-some and fair, Kin we git
larg - in' here, o here, Kin we git larg - in' here?

2 This is my daughter and she sets by my side,
And none of you hog drovers kin have her for
                              your bride,
And you can't git largin' here, o here,
And you can't git largin' here.

3 Don't care for your daughter, much less for
                              yourself,
We'll go on a piece further and better ourselves
And we don't want largin', etc.

4 Gold miners, gold miners, etc.

5 This is my daughter and she sets by my side,
And one of you miners kin have her for
                              your bride,
By bringing another one here, o here,
By bringing another one here.

6 Cowboys, cowboys, etc.

7 This is my daughter and she sets
                         in my lap
And none of you cowboys kin take her from
                         her pap, etc.

"Hog Drovers" from *The Folk Songs of North America* by Alan Lomax. Used by permission of The Richmond Organization, New York.

An Early Stage

As the expanding country outgrew its packhorse trails, more paths were widened and more stumps were pulled until freight wagons and stagecoaches were rolling west on turnpikes everywhere. The mail coach drivers were the Kings of the road. Mail coaches, drawn by spans, or pairs, of fancy coach horses, and driven by swaggering "jehus," always created excitement as they passed. When their echoing horns blew, people moved out of the way fast! This gave rise to the saying, "The United States mail must go through." Have you ever heard this saying?

Conestoga freight wagons with wheels higher than a man's head raised dust all day on these roads. They rolled from dawn to dark at a slow steady pace. The great blue wagons with white canvas tops and red sides were named for the Pennsylvania Valley where they first were built in 1725. Conestoga wagons carried most of the freight and passengers that went westward over the Alleghenies from the time of the Revolutionary War until about 1850.

The freight drivers were called "wagoners." They had a lot in common with sailors on the lumbering, "wind-jammer" vessels. Tough, rough, and ready for anything, they drove all day in sun, rain or snow. At night they unhitched their horses and tied them to the long wagon-tongues in the wagon yards at inns or taverns along the road. These wayside wagon yards were crowded with rowdy drivers chewing tobacco, smoking Marsh-Wheeling stogies and spinning yarns about their overland adventures.

The professional wagoners had an important part in the building of America. They carried thousands and thousands of pioneer families over the Appalachian passes to the new lands in the mid-west, and they freighted supplies for the new settlements growing there. They had to face Indians, wild animals, washouts, landslides, outlaws, and, perhaps worst of all—mud. Although they spent more time in lifting their wagons out of mud holes and shouting orders to their horses or oxen than in singing, the tunes that they did sing were plentiful and boisterous. Here is one of their favorite tunes, *The Jolly Wagoner*. It was still being sung not many years ago in Pennsylvania. As you sing this tune, try to imagine that you are driving a Conestoga wagon.

The Jolly Wagoner

When I first went a-wag-on-ing, a-wag-on-ing did go,— I
filled my par-ents' hearts full of sor-row, grief and woe,— And man-y are the
hard-ships that I have since gone through.— Sing wo, my lads, sing wo;— drive
on, my lads, I oh! Who would-n't lead the life of a jol-ly wag-on-er?—

Stagecoach Travel

The driver was called a stage driver because he traveled in "stages." Each stage was equal to a day's journey, and, for this same reason, the coaches in which passengers rode were called stagecoaches. The men who drove them had to be bold, expert and iron-nerved. Since stagecoaches carried the valuable express of the day as well as the United States mail, the drivers also had to be trustworthy.

The arrival of a stagecoach in a frontier town or at a relay station provided a moment of pause for everyone except the stablemen. The horses were beautiful animals, lighter and more swift than the wagon horses. They were cared for in stables, and every twelve miles or so a fresh team of six horses awaited the coach.

After driving to the station at full speed, the driver stopped in the road with a screech of the brakes. He threw down his reins and remained on the high seat. The horse-tenders unhitched the team and put in fresh horses. The reins were thrown back to the driver. Off he went, driving at full speed again.

When the stagecoach driver stopped for the night at an inn or tavern he was received as an important person. He was dapper in his dress and confident in his manner. Regarded as a trusted friend by many travelers, he was the envy of every young boy along the turnpike.

"Pike boys" all wanted to grow up to be racing stagecoach drivers, the way so many boys today want to be airplane pilots or astronauts.

Inns and Taverns

The untamed country, savage as when Columbus landed, stretched into the west for nearly three thousand miles. But the turnpikes reaching out from the Atlantic states were threads of civilization in the wilderness. A few miles to either side of the roads, Indians prowled and wolves howled. But within the snug confines of roadside hostelries, travelers could relax. They could *almost* imagine they were back home.

As more and more people went west, the number of inns and taverns increased until along the more important roads you could find one about every twelve miles. Usually these were long houses built of logs or stone, fronting on the road. They were managed by genial men who gave travelers a hearty welcome.

Sleeping accomodations were not the finest in the world, but they served the purpose. Mattresses stuffed with straw or corn shucks were standard. But there were feather beds for people who could pay more — and a place in front of a roaring twelve-foot log fire where those with lean pocketbooks could spread their blankets on the floor. Late-comers often had no choice but to sleep on the floor, even at the best inns. People with no money at all to spend for lodging, camped along the road, sleeping in their wagons or under them.

Although tableware was scarce, the food was plentiful. Everything to eat was put on a long table, and table manners were not exactly delicate. The traveler paid a fee of a few cents and ate all he wanted of roast coon, wild turkey, venison, pork or fresh river fish.

A Stagecoach and an Inn

Evenings at roadside inns were loud and merry, with story-telling and singing. Travelers told of their experiences far and wide. Adventurers who had reached the very edge of the frontier and were returning to move their families west described the new lands. They sometimes bragged and told tall tales. Good story-tellers, or yarn-spinners, often were asked to tell a ghost story. Here is a story that was told by people from the New England states. As you read the story, see if you can find the clue as to what had happened to Peter Rugg.

Peter Rugg

In the summer of 1820 I took the stagecoach from Providence to Boston where I had business. All other seats being taken, I accepted the place next to the driver, a pleasant and civil fellow. We had proceeded some ten miles when suddenly the horses laid their ears back on their necks, like hares, and the driver asked if I had a raincoat with me.

"No," said I, "why do you ask?"

"The horses see the 'storm breeder'," he replied, "and we shall see him soon."

I looked at him curiously. There was not a cloud in the sky, much less any suggestion of a storm. All I could see was a tiny speck, far down the road.

"There comes the storm breeder," said the driver.

The speck became a carriage drawn by a black horse and carrying a little girl and a man. The man, who was driving very fast, looked oddly at us as we passed. When he had gone by, our horses' ears rose up again, and I inquired who the man was.

"Nobody knows," said the driver, "but I've met him and the child before. I've been asked the way to Boston so often by that man, even when he was traveling directly away from it, as he was now, that I have finally refused to talk to him."

"Does he never stop anywhere?"

"No longer than to inquire the way to Boston. He always says he has to reach Boston by nightfall."

We had reached the top of a high hill near Walpole, and I commented to the driver about how clear the heavens were. But when we topped yet another hill, he pointed to the east, and I saw a little black seed cloud no bigger than a hat. "You have to look in the direction whence the man came," he said. "A horrible storm always follows him. I hope we reach Polley's tavern before it reaches us."

The horses, without being urged, increased their pace, and the little cloud boiled up into a big black one. Just as we reached Polley's, the rain poured down in torrents!

Soon afterward, a gentleman who had been traveling behind us arrived. Then came a peddler. Some of my fellow passengers asked the newcomers if they had seen the man with the little girl. Both of them had.

"He asked me the way to Boston," said the gentleman, "and the moment he went on, a thunderclap broke over his head and his horse sprang forward. They seemed to travel as fast as the thundercloud!"

"I've met that man in four different states," the peddler added. "Each time, a thundershower soaked me, and my horse behaved in a curiously frightened way."

When the weather improved, I went on, and I gradually forgot about the mysterious traveler. Three years went by. And then, the other day, I was standing outside Bennett's Hotel in Hartford and heard a man say, "There goes Peter Rugg and his child — farther from Boston than ever." And there, driving past me, wet and weary, and with the same child and black horse, was the man I had seen three years before.

"And who is Peter Rugg?" I asked.

"That is more than anyone can tell exactly," said the man. "He is a famous traveler who is not liked by innkeepers, for he never stops to eat, drink or sleep. I wonder why the government does not employ him to carry the mail."

"Ay, and how long would it take him to get a letter to Boston?" said a sarcastic bystander.

"But does he never stop anywhere?" I asked. "Please, sir, tell me about Rugg."

The man looked at me uneasily. "Sir," he said, "those who know the most about him say the least. I'll tell you this much. The last time Rugg inquired of me how far it was to Boston, I told him 100 miles. 'Why,' said he, 'how can you deceive me so? It is cruel to mislead a traveler.' I repeated that it was 100 miles. 'How can you say so?' he cried out. 'I was told last evening it was but 50, and I have been traveling all night.' I told him he had been traveling *away* from Boston, and to turn around and go back the other direction. 'Alas,' said he, 'it is always turn back! Boston shifts with the wind and the signposts, too. They all point the wrong way. And it has been foul weather ever since I left home.' I invited him then to stop and rest. 'No,' said he, 'I must reach home tonight. I think you must be mistaken in the distance to Boston.'"

That was all this man would tell me. But just as my luck would have it, the black horse, carriage, man and child returned down the street. They would have passed, but I was determined to speak to Peter Rugg, or whoever he might be. I stepped into the street, and the man stopped his horse.

"Sir," said I, "may I be so bold as to inquire if you are not Mr. Rugg?"

"Indeed, I am," he said. "My name is Peter Rugg. I have lost my way. I am wet and weary."

"You live in Boston, do you not? And in what street?"

"In Middle Street. Number 23."

"How did you and your child become so wet? It has not rained here today."

"It has just rained a heavy shower up the river. Would you advise me to take the old road to Boston or the turnpike?"

"Why, the old road is 117 miles, and the turnpike is 97."

"You are teasing me. You know it is but 40 miles from Newburyport to Boston."

"But this is not Newburyport. It is Hartford."

"Do not deceive me, sir. Is not this town Newburyport and the river the Merrimac?"

"No, sir; this is Hartford and the river the Connecticut."

He dropped the reins and wrung his hands. "Have the rivers, too, changed their courses as the cities have changed places? Ah, that fatal oath!" His impatient horse leaped off.

But I had discovered a clue to the history of Peter Rugg. When business next called me to Boston, I went to 23 Middle Street and talked with a Mrs. Croft, an aged lady who had lived in the house, she said, for the last 20 years.

She said that once every year on the 13th of November a stranger stopped at her door. He came in an old carriage with a black horse and a small child, and he asked for Mrs. Rugg.

Upon being told she did not live here now, the stranger always said sadly, "Though the paint is rather faded, this looks like my house."

And the little girl always added, "Yes, that is the stone before the door that I used to sit on to eat my bread and milk."

"But," said the stranger, "it seems to be on the wrong side of the street. Indeed, everything seems misplaced. Has John Foy come home from sea?"

"Sir," said Mrs. Croft, "I have never heard of John Foy. Where did he live?"

"In Orange Tree Lane, just above here."

"There is no such lane now."

The stranger seemed confused. "Strange mistake! How much this looks like the town of Boston!"

"Why, this *is* Boston," Mrs. Croft told him.

His horse began to paw the pavement. The stranger, clearly bewildered, said vaguely, "No home tonight." Giving reins to his horse, he disappeared down the street . . .

Now, while Mrs. Croft was telling me these things, an elderly neighbor had stopped to listen. "I knew Peter Rugg," he told me. "And I tell you it is impossible that you could have seen him *with* his child. Jenny Rugg, if living, is now about — let's see, the Boston Massacre was in 1770 — is now more than 60 years of age. Peter, himself, would be about 90."

"Sir," I addressed the neighbor, "tell me what you know of Peter Rugg."

And this is what he told me:

"Peter Rugg was a man with plenty of money and well-respected. But, unhappily, his temper was dreadful, and then his language was terrible. If a door stood in his way, he would kick the

panels through. At moments of terrible anger he would swear so much that his wig would arise from his head. He had no respect for heaven or earth.

"One evening — a November 13th, it was — Rugg was returning in his chaise with his daughter from Concord. A storm overtook them, and at dark he stopped at Menotomy, now West Cambridge, at the home of a friend. The friend, a Mr. Cutter, urged him to stop overnight because the tempest was increasing.

" 'Let the storm increase', said Rugg with a fearful oath. 'I will see home tonight in spite of the tempest, or may I never see home!'

"At these words he whipped his high-spirited black horse and disappeared in a moment. But Peter Rugg did not reach home that night or the next. He was never traced beyond Mr. Cutter's in Menotomy. But for a long time after, on every dark and stormy night, his wife and their neighbors heard the crack of his whip and the rattling of his carriage past their doors. The clatter shook the houses on both sides of the street.

"There were stories that he was seen in various places, but the more his friends inquired, the more they were puzzled. If they heard of Rugg one day in Connecticut, the next day they heard of him winding around the hills in New Hampshire. A toll-collector at Charlestown Bridge said that about the time Rugg was first missing, on dark and stormy nights, a horse and carriage would roar over the bridge at midnight, loud as a troop, completely ignoring the toll or fee that should have been paid for crossing the bridge. This happened so often that the toll-collector, when next he saw the same horse and carriage approaching the bridge from Charlestown Square, took his stand holding a large three-legged stool in his hand. As the black horse and carriage rolled past, he hurled the stool. The Tollman said the stool went right through the horse. Thereafter, he seemed anxious not to talk about Peter Rugg. And Rugg, his child, his horse and carriage remain a mystery to this day."

Sometimes during an evening at an inn, travelers would sing and dance. Play-party songs were popular. *In the Wilderness* was one of the songs that was sung on such occasions. Can you create a dance to this song? Read the words carefully.

In The Wilderness

1. First lit-tle la-dy in the wil-der-ness In the wil-der-ness, in the wil-der-ness, First lit-tle la-dy in the wil-der-ness On to Ga-li-lee.

CHORUS
Hands up, round the la-dy, round the la-dy, Round the la-dy, On to Ga-li-lee.

2 Swing that lady out of the wilderness, etc.

3 Next old married lady go down the wilderness, etc.

4 Next old maid go down the wilderness, etc.

5 Swing all the ladies out of the wilderness, etc.

6 First old hobo in the wilderness, etc.

7 First old gentleman in the wilderness, etc.

CHILDREN CAN MAKE UP MORE VERSES.

If the area around the inn was at all "settled-up," and if land had been cleared along the turnpike for farms, the young folks among the travelers might ride bareback to a schoolhouse dance, a box-supper, or a spelling bee. But no matter what the activity, the inn-keeper awakened travelers at an early hour the next morning by blowing on a conch shell or ringing a bell. Everyone hurried outside to wash in the horse trough, then rushed back in for breakfast. There was a great rustling around and clanking in the wagon yard as horses were harnessed. By daylight, everyone was on the road west again.

"In the Wilderness" by Alan Lomax. Used by permission of Ludlow Music, Inc., New York.

Adventures Along the Natchez Trace

Some early roads and trails had places for travelers to stay that were surprisingly different from those along the turnpikes. On the "bloody" Natchez Trace, or trail, the inns for a time were controlled and run by Indians. From Natchez, on the Mississippi River, to Nashville, the lands over which this Trace ran belonged to Choctaw and Chickasaw Indians who were jealous of the use of their ancient warrior trail. By keeping control of the river ferries and most of the inns, they hoped to keep the white men from taking their land.

The Natchez Trace was well-named, because that's all it was — a trace, a dim line of travel through deep woods and dark cane breaks.

On the Natchez Trace

With the tide of western travel swelling into the lower Mississippi basin, Natchez became an important center for both land and water traffic. Settlers in the middle states floated their farm products south by water to sell at New Orleans. Many preferred the risk of returning home by land over the Natchez Trace rather than by the long, hard, push-and-pull against the up-river current.

The risk was from outlaws. Since nearly everybody who went north carried money, outlaws infested the lonesome trail in appalling numbers. The Natchez Trace was probably the most perilous route of travel east of the Mississippi. The bush outlaws who rode it, or the dry-land pirates as they were sometimes called, were merciless.

You may have heard of John Murrell, the "most tarnal villain of all." He is said to have murdered more than a hundred men whom he robbed on the Trace, and at the time of his own death he had well-organized plans for establishing an outright "outlaw empire" in the southern states in defiance of federal authority.

"I never rob but I kill," he is quoted as saying. "Dead men never get their money back."

To protect themselves, prudent men traveled in well-armed parties of from five to twenty-five in number. The inns were far apart on the Natchez Trace, and some of them were little safer than the trail through the dark crackling cane. Some, in fact, were actually operated by outlaws, and many a story was told in those days of unwary travelers murdered in their corn-husk beds.

For all this, when travelers reached one of the inns in numbers large enough to feel safe, they might celebrate their good fortune by singing and dancing to such old tunes as *Weevily Wheat*. This old tune originated in England in about 1745. It was brought to America by the early settlers, and, as a play-party song, it was heard on many frontiers.

Weevily Wheat

I don't want none of your weev-i-ly wheat, I don't want none of your bar-ley, I want some flour and half an hour To bake a cake for Char-lie.

Settlers in "Old Kaintuck"

Once the Indian menace became less, settlers poured over Boone's Trace into the rich land of Kentucky. They took what land they wanted and marked its boundaries by blazing or chipping the bark of "witness trees." Such land claims were sometimes called "tomahawk claims." Many people lost their land by failing to register their claims with government land offices. In fact, Daniel Boone was one of these people.

Many men besides Daniel Boone became famous as Indian fighters. They were rough, tough men who had to make their own laws in a land where there were no laws. As a community became "settled-up," these "ring-tail roarers" moved out and took their "outlandish" ideas with them. People never forgot them, however, and their exploits became part of our frontier folklore.

Such a man was Davy Crockett, who used to brag that he was "half horse, half alligator, and able to whip his weight in wild cats." Tall tales were told about Davy's prowess as a hunter and backwoodsman. Supposedly, he wrote some of these tales himself. Here is one of them.

Sunrise in His Pocket

by Davy Crockett

One January morning it was so all-screwen-up cold that the forest trees war so stiff that they couldn't shake, and the very day-break froze fast as it war tryin' to dawn. The tinder-box in my cabin would no more ketch fire than a sunk raft at the bottom o' the sea. Seein' that daylight war so far behind time, I thought creation war in a fair way for freezin' fast.

"So," thinks I, "I must strike a leetle fire from my fingers, light my pipe, travel out a few leagues, and see about it."

Then I brought my knuckles together like two thunder clouds, but the sparks froze up afore I could begin to collect 'em—so out I walked, and endeavored to keep myself unfriz by goin' at a hop, step and jump gait, and whistlin' the tune of *Fire in the Mountains* as I went along in three double quick time. Well, arter I had walked about twenty-five miles up the peak o' Daybreak Hill, I soon discovered what war the matter. The airth had actually friz fast in her axis, and couldn't turn round; the sun had got jammed between two cakes o'

Davy Crockett   Los Angeles County Museum

ice under the wheels, an' thar he had bin shinin' and workin' to get loose, till he friz fast in his cold sweat.

"C-r-e-a-t-i-o-n!" thought I, "this are the toughest sort o' suspension, and it mustn't be undured—somethin' must be done, or human creation is done for."

It war then so antedeluvian and premature cold that my upper and lower teeth an' tongue war all collapsed together as tight as a friz oyster. I took a fresh twenty-ton bear off o' my back that I'd picked up on the road, an' beat the animal agin the ice till the hot ile began to walk out on him at all sides. I then took an' held him over the airth's axes, an' squeezed him till I thaw'd 'em loose, poured about a ton on it over the sun's face, give the airth's cogwheel one kick backward till I got the sun loose, whistled *Push along, keep movin'* an' in about fifteen seconds the airth gin a grunt, and begun movin'. The sun walked up beautiful then, salutin' me with sich a wind o' gratitude that it made me sneeze. I lit my pipe by the blaze o' his topknot, shouldered my bear, an' walked home, introducin' the people to fresh daylight with a piece of sunrise in my pocket, with which I cooked my bear steaks, an' enjoyed one o' the best breakfasts I had tasted for some time. If I didn't, jist wake some mornin' and go with me to the office o' sunrise!

When Davy Crockett went to Congress in 1827, he had the reputation of being a very remarkable hunter. In Washington he became a half-comic superhero as the politicians made him appear in this next tale on page 32.

Davy Crockett's Boast

I'm that same David Crockett, fresh from the backwoods, half horse, half alligator, a little touched with the snapping turtle; can wade the Mississippi, leap the Ohio, ride upon a streak of lightning, and slip without a scratch down a honey locust; can whip my weight in wildcats—and if any gentleman pleases, for a ten dollar bill, he may throw in a panther—hug a bear too close for comfort, and eat any man opposed to Jackson.

I had taken old Betsy and straggled off to the banks of the Mississippi River; and meeting with no game, I didn't like it a bit. I felt mighty wolfish about the head and ears, and thought I would spile if I wasn't kivured up in salt, for I hadn't had a fight in anyway 10 days; and I cum acrost a fellow floatin' down stream settin' in the stern of his boat fast asleep.

Said I, "Hello, stranger! If you don't take keer your boat will run away with you." He looked up and said he, "I don't value you." He looked up at me slantendicler, and I looked down upon him slantendicler; and he took out a chew of turbaccur and held it up, and said he, "I don't value you *that*."

Said I "Cum ashore, I can whip you —I've been trying to git a fight all the mornin'."

The varmint flapped his wings and crowed like a chicken. I ris up, shook my mane, and neighed like a horse. He run his boat plump head foremost ashore. I stood still waitin for him and sot my triggurs, that is, took off my shurt, and tied my galluses tight around my waist—and at it we went.

He was a right smart fellur, but hardly a bait for such a fellur as me. I put it to him mightly droll. In 10 minutes he yelled enough, and swore I was a ripstavur.

Said I, "Ain't I the yaller flower of the forest! And I am all brimstone but the head and ears, and that's aquafortis."

Said he, "Stranger, you are a beauty; and if I know'd your name, I'd vote for you next election."

Said I, "I'm that same David Crockett. You know what I'm made of. I've got the closest shootin' rifle, the best 'coon dog, and the ruffest racking horse in the district. I can fool more varmints, and cool out more men than any man you can find in all Kentucky."

Said he, "Good mornin, stranger—I'm satisfied."

Said I, "Good mornin, sir; I feel much better since our meetin." But after I got away a piece I said, "Hello, friend, don't forget that vote."

From the tale you just read, you know that Davy Crockett's gun was always a part of his attire. After you study the painting on page 30, you might want to find out more about the kind of gun Davy Crockett used and the kind of clothing worn at that time. Where do you suppose pioneers learned how to make clothing of buckskin? Do you know what animal's skin is used to make this kind of clothing? What kind of animal's skin is used to make the kind of hat in the painting?

"Davy Crockett's Boast" reprinted by permission of Time and Life Books, Inc., from *The Treasury of American Folklore* by the Editors of Time-Life, Inc., copyright 1961.

Many funny stories were told about buckskin clothing because it became so stiff when wet and cold. And it was hot in the summer. However, it was strong and lasted a long time. In this story, you can read about how tough and strong buckskin pants could be.

Stump Pulling Pants

Everybody knows that the early pioneers and plainsmen wore clothes of buckskin. This was not only because cloth was hard to get, but because buckskin, although soft and comfortable, will stand great wear and tear. But if you doubt this tall tale about the strength of buckskin told by an old settler, you will be excused:

"I was breaking sod in Northern Texas with four yoke of oxen," he drawled. "Something frightened them, and we started on a dead run straight for a big sycamore stump at least five feet in diameter.

"Well, sir, the plow struck it about in the center and split it wide open. I was still clinging to the handles of the plow, which went clean through the stump, dragging me after. The stump flew together again and caught me by the seat of my buckskin pants."

"What happened then?" asked one of the bewildered listeners.

"Well, sir, would you believe it? My pants pulled that stump clean out by the roots."

A Frontier Cabin

"Stump Pulling Pants" adapted from "Tough Buckskin" in *A Treasury of Western Folklore*, edited by B. A. Botkin. New York: Crown Publishers, Inc., 1951.

Daily Life of the Kentucky Settler

In the first Kentucky cabins, the people were far from any place where they could buy supplies, so they had to make everything they needed. Salt was made by boiling the water from salt springs. Saltpeter, found in caves, was ground to make gunpowder.

Some of the things that people do today as hobbies were done to provide the necessities of life on the frontier. Pioneer women first had to spin the thread and weave the cloth they would use later to make clothing for their families.

The men planted flax as soon as enough land was cleared. From the fibers of this plant, linen thread was spun. The preparation of flax for spinning was very difficult. The woody parts had to be broken into small bits. Broken flax still had to be "swingled" to knock the bits of stalk out of the fiber. Flax swingling was one of the chores for which neighbors gathered to help. They would sing as they worked to make the work easier and more fun. They might sing a song like *Go Tell Aunt Rhody*.

Go Tell Aunt Rhody

1. Go tell Aunt Rho - dy, — go tell Aunt Rho - dy, —
Go tell Aunt Rho - dy the old gray goose is dead.

2. The one she'd been saving, the one she'd been saving,
The one she'd been saving to make a feather bed.

3. He died a kicking, he died a kicking,
He died a kicking to make a feather bed.

To get the very last impurities from the flax, the fibers were pulled through smaller and smaller "hetchels." These were pieces of wood through which iron spikes had been driven. The linen that the coarsest hetchel caught could be used to make sacking and canvas. The next grade was the scratchy linen used for men's work clothes.

Last of all was the long, pure fiber used for women's and children's clothes and for men's Sunday shirts. The women spun all three kinds on "the little wheel," as the flax wheel was called.

These spinning wheels were made by the settlers. The "linen spinner" sat at her work with her right foot operating a treadle that turned the wheel. The important skill in spinning was to feed the new fiber by hand to the spindle. This had to be done smoothly so there would be no lumps or weak spots in the thread.

Most settlers raised several sheep for their wool. Usually a sheep is sheared, and then the wool is washed. However, in "Old Kaintuck" the animals were washed in a pond and then sheared. The job of picking out burrs was a troublesome one which the children often did. The women carded the wool into pieces, or "slivers," by dragging it between two wooden cards that had short wire teeth. The finished slivers were eight or ten inches long, light and fluffy, and they came to points at each end. They were spun into yarn on "the big wheel" that the spinner turned by hand as she stood at her work. The yarn was tied into "hanks" before it was removed from the reel.

Most weaving of cloth was done at home on barn-frame looms made by settlers. Very little all-wool cloth was woven. Combining wool and linen threads produced a kind of "linsey-woolsey" cloth. This cloth lasted longer than wool because of the strong linen thread.

Thread was dyed with colors that were made from materials found in the woods. Brown-yellow was produced by boiling the inner-bark of the white walnut tree. A rusty black dye was made from black walnut shells. Blue was made from the bark of the blue ash tree.

Unless the cloth was "fulled" first, woolen garments shrank. Fulling, or preshrinking, thickened and strengthened the material. Settlers had fulling parties. At such a party the new cloth was first soaked in hot soapsuds and then thrown on the split-log floor of a cabin. The guests, sitting in a circle on stools, stomped on the wet cloth with their bare feet as they sang and told stories and jokes. After the party, the cloth was rinsed and hung on a shady fence to dry.

Splint brooms were made by the men. The wood was stripped back from one end in thin splints a foot or more long. When the heart of the log was reached, it was cut out entirely. More splints were shoved down, leaving their lower ends attached just above the tops of the first bunch. The upper splints were then bent down over the lower ones and tied. When the rest of the upper part of the log had been cut down to handle-size, the broom was finished.

While men did such things as making brooms during the long winter evenings, the women worked at tasks like spinning and weaving. The older children shelled corn. Babies sometimes amused themselves by playing with the empty corn cobs.

Most of the light by which families worked during the evening was provided by the fire in the fireplace. However, some crude candles called "tallow dips" were used to give extra light. Some people even made a kind of "boat lamp." This was a shallow dish filled with grease, which burned by means of a wick. In reality, more foul-smelling smoke than light was created by this kind of lamp.

The men of the family were good craftsmen because everything used in the home had to be made from materials that they could find around them. Wooden churns were fashioned by hand. Children helped with the churning of butter, which was made from cream. You may remember that cows were among the animals that were driven over the Wilderness Trail.

In pioneer days you could not go to a store and buy soap as we do. The housewife had to make her own soap from grease and wood ash lye. Salt was needed to harden the soap, and since salt was scarce, most people used soap in its soft state. It was very coarse and slimy. It would not feel anything like the soap we use to day.

Wash day was a long, tiring time for the mother. Water had to be carried in homemade wooden buckets and heated in a big iron pot over an outdoor fire. After pounding the clothes against a stump with a wooden paddle to get the dirt out, they were rinsed and hung on the fence to dry. Few mothers did any ironing. Those who did iron heated a "sadiron" on the fireplace hearth by turning its underside toward the fire. They used a "puncheon," or split-log bench, for an ironing board.

Many people today collect and treasure things that were made by the early pioneers. They know that all members of the pioneer family had to work together to provide the necessities of life. These things that were made by pioneer fathers required many hours of patient work.

Maple syrup, maple sugar and honey were the common "sweetnin's" for the Kentucky pioneer. Every farmer had a grove of maple trees, and sugaring was an early spring job of men and boys.

First, they tapped the trees with an axe and drove "spiles" into the cuts. All day while the sun was shining on the trees, the maple sap dripped from the spiles into "gathering buckets." At dusk, the sap was collected in a barrel tied on a sled. The sled was dragged to the fire, and the sap was emptied into a big iron pot where it was boiled all night to evaporate most of the water and make syrup. Some of the syrup was boiled longer and made into maple sugar.

Men and boys got little sleep during sugaring time, but no one minded. This was a time for fun and "good tasting." At night, everyone sat around the fire and told stories and sang songs. Some of the songs were sad, while others were very gay. As you read the words of these two songs, decide whether they make you feel happy or sad.

Black Is the Color of My True Love's Hair

Plaintively

Girls: 1. Black, black, black is the col-or of my true love's hair,

His face is hand-some, ros-y fair, The sweet-est face,

the neat est hands, I love the ground where-on he stands.

Boys: 2 Winter's passed and the tender maple leaves are green,
The time is gone that we have seen, But still I hope,
now spring is here, That you and I no more need fear.

Girls: 3 True it is that I love my love and well he knows
I love the ground whereon he goes;
If you no more on earth I see,
I can't serve you as you have me.

Boys: 4 I will go to the river just to moan and weep;
For sad at heart I ne'er could sleep.
I'll write to you a few short lines;
I'll suffer death ten thousand times.

All: 5 Fare you well, fare you well again, my own true love.
The day is done, I wish you well;
And still I hope the time will come
When once again we'll see the sun.

Sourwood Mountain

With lively movement

1. Chick-en crow-ing on Sour-wood Moun-tain, Hey de-ing dang did-dle al-ly day.

So man-y pret-ty girls, I can't count 'em, Hey de-ing dang did-dle al-ly day.

My true love, she lives in Letch-er, Hey de-ing dang did-dle al-ly day.

She won't come, and I won't fetch her, Hey de-ing dang did-dle al-ly day.

2 My true love's a blue-eyed daisy,
If I don't get her, I'll go crazy,
Big dog bark, and little one bite you,
Big girl'll court, and little one'll slight you,

3 My true love lives up the river,
A few more jumps and I'll be with her,
My true love lives in the hollow,
She won't come, and I won't follow,

Besides syrup and sugar made from the sap of maple trees, another sweet-nin' used by the pioneers was honey. Many bees were brought to America by the English colonists. As the bees became greater in number, they spread westward. Frontiersmen hunted their hives to get the honey. Men and boys learned how to observe and follow the flight pattern of bees so that they could locate the hive, which was usually in a hollow tree. When a "bee tree" was robbed, the honey was shared with the neighbors who had helped to get the honey.

"Sourwood Mountain" from *Voices of America* by Wolfe, Krone, and Fullerton. Follett Publishing Company, copyright 1963.

Corn Husking Bee

Corn was the most important crop raised in Kentucky. At harvest time the ears were pulled from the corn stalks and heaped in a long pile for a corn-husking bee.

All the men and boys in a neighborhood gathered for the corn husking. It began at dusk with the choosing of two team captains. The captains placed a fence rail across the pile of corn at a point they agreed was its middle. Teams were chosen. Taking the covering off the ears of corn, or husking, began in the middle of the pile. Each team tried to undermine the rail and make it fall to its side. This would lengthen the pile for the other team. Once the rail was on the ground, both teams raced to win. They worked with a kind of rhythmic chant that could be heard for at least a mile on a still night. A shout hailed the winning side. The winners, with their captains held high on their shoulders, paraded around and around the losers. Then everybody sat down to a pot-pie supper that had been prepared by the women and girls.

Taking corn to the mill to be ground was usually a boy's job. It might be a trip of ten miles or more. If the boy waited for the grinding to be done, he might be gone all day. Sometimes the miller would just take meal from his own stack and give it to the boy. Then the boy did not need to wait for the grinding to be done. The miller held out a tenth part of the meal for his grinding fee.

Special Craftsmen Come to the Frontier

With the coming of more and more settlers to the frontier, villages often grew up around forts and mills, or perhaps at a spot where two trails crossed. It was also important for the village to be located close to a salt spring. A village serving as a trading place for several hundred families would commonly have a meeting house or church, a burial ground in the churchyard, a store and two taverns. Different kinds of craftsmen, or workers, gradually moved into the village to do the things that people needed to have done.

A very important man in any frontier community was the blacksmith. Part of his job was to shoe horses. As you look at this picture, you can see some of the things that had to be done in shoeing a horse.

The Blacksmith

A carpenter made coffins in addition to building other kinds of things.

The blacksmith was also a gunsmith and a wheel-maker.

The cobbler who made and mended boots and shoes served as a harness-maker, too.

Animal skins were made into leather by another kind of craftsman called a tanner.

Barrels, pails and tubs were made by a cooper. "Wet," or watertight, barrels were needed to hold liquids such as molasses. "Dry" barrels that were not watertight were needed to hold flour and other ground materials. Barrel staves were rough planks cut from logs. The skilled cooper, or barrel-maker, shaped the staves into barrels, tubs and buckets. He placed at least two hoops around the shaped staves to hold them in place.

After 1790, frontier village stores had a few grocery items, drugs, hardware, cloth, hats, leather goods, books, writing paper, and of course, ammunition for guns.

Bibles, hymn books, and perhaps a few copies of *Pilgrim's Progress* were for sale.

Slates and slate pencils were sold for school use. In addition, primers, spellers, arithmetic books and almanacs were available.

No family would think of trying to get along without a copy of *Poor Richard's Almanac*. This was a kind of book in which Benjamin Franklin listed the phases of the moon, along with other information. Pioneers believed that seeds had to be planted when the phases of the moon were just right, or the seeds would not grow. The *Almanac* also included many sayings that people still remember today. After you have read these, see if you can think of others.

Lost time is never found again.

He that riseth late, must trot all day.

Early to bed, and early to rise, makes a man healthy, wealthy, and wise.

If we are industrious, we shall never starve.

Plough deep, while sluggards sleep, and you shall have corn to sell and to keep.

Be ashamed to catch yourself idle.

Most purchases in the village general store were paid for with corn, hay, eggs, or home products such as maple sugar or barrel staves. When any real money changed hands, it was paper money. If there was no other way to make change, it was done by the "cut money" method. This meant that a piece equal to the change needed was cut from the paper money. What do you think would happen if a storekeeper tried to make change in this manner today?

Saturday was a time for fun and contests among the men. They enjoyed races of all kinds. They liked to race their horses. The owner of the fastest running horse was very proud.

Good hunting dogs were very important since the pioneers depended on hunting for most of their meat. Men had contests with their hunting dogs to see which dog could best follow an animal's trail. They sometimes took a wild animal, such as a fox, over a very tricky trail that criss-crossed and doubled back. Then they turned the dogs loose to see if they could follow the trail. The men loved their dogs and really felt sad if something happened to one of them. This song tells about the sadness of the owner of *Old Blue*.

Old Blue

Moderately

Had a dog and his name was Blue, Had a dog and his name was Blue.

Had a dog and his name was Blue, Bet-cha five dol-ars he's a good 'un too. —

Here, _____ Blue, _____ you

good dog ___ you _____

Coda for last verse

Ev-ery link I'd call his name,

Here, _____ Blue, _____ You

good dog _____ you. _____

2. Shouldered my gun and I tooted my horn,
   Gonna find a 'possum in the new-ground corn,
   Old Blue barked and I went to see,
   Cornered a 'possum up in a tree.

   Come on Blue, you good dog, you.

3. Old Blue died, and he died so hard,
   Shook the ground in my back yard,
   Dug his grave with a silver spade,
   Lowered him down with links of chain.

   Every link, I did call his name,
   Here Blue, you good dog, you,
   Here Blue, I'm a-comin' there too.

"Old Blue" from *The Joan Baez Songbook*. Reprinted by permission, Ryerson Music Publishers, Inc.

All the excitement from the Saturday contests and fun disappeared in the peace of Sunday morning. Families walked or rode their horses to the meeting house or church. Everyone was scrubbed clean and dressed up. The men polished their boots with soot from the fireplace which had been mixed with bear grease! They wore their best clothes. Women and girls dressed in calico, a kind of printed cotton cloth. The women usually wore black silk bonnets over a white linen cap, with tabs that tied under the chin. Boys and girls almost always went barefoot in the summertime, even if they were wearing their best clothes.

There was a time for visiting before church. After the morning service, people sat together and talked as they ate their picnic lunches. In the afternoon they attended another service in the church. Children sat with their parents through both long church sessions.

A Frontier School

Let's look at how *different* schools were in frontier days. For one thing, you didn't *have* to go. As early as 1787, there were schools in "Old Kaintuck" but when there was work to be done at home, children stayed home to help their parents. Schoolmasters were almost always men. As a rule, they didn't stay very long in one place, and when a schoolmaster left, the school was closed until another could be hired.

Classes were held in a log cabin. To get light into the room, cracks were left between logs, and the cracks covered with oiled paper. Children of all ages sat on split logs that had been smoothed to make "puncheon benches." Often younger children could not reach the floor with their feet, but they were required to sit still and study aloud. Pupils were called to the front of the room when it was time for recitation, since every pupil was required to recite his lessons aloud for the teacher. See what other differences you can find by looking at the picture of a pioneer school room on page 47.

Before the McGuffey Readers were available, the New Testament of the Bible served as a reader for the children.

At the end of each day, the teacher held a "spell-down" that lasted until only one pupil was left standing. This pupil became the spelling champion until the next spelldown or spelling-bee.

A pupil was expected to practice good manners at school, or he was spanked by the schoolmaster. Then it was likely that he would be spanked again at home for getting into trouble at school!

This picture of a later frontier school shows that children of all ages attended the same one-room school.

A One-room School   Utah Historical Society

Kentucky pioneers never missed a chance to combine fun with their work. You have read about the corn husking and cloth fulling parties. Another time when neighbors got together for combined work and play was at a "quilting party." A bed quilt was made by sewing scraps of cloth together to form geometric patterns. Some quilt designs were especially pretty. Some patterns created by pioneer women are shown on page 49. Perhaps your parents own a quilt that was made long ago. See if it has a design like one of these.

After the ladies had sewed and gossiped, supper was served, and there was always much singing. Sometimes a traveling singing teacher held classes at such social gatherings. Here is a song that was popular at quilting bees. Try to imagine that you can hear the fiddle as it sounded at a pioneer party. Have you discovered that "fiddle" is a common name for the violin? The fiddle was about the only musical instrument on the frontier for many years.

Uncle Joe

Rollicking   VERSE

1. Did you ev-er go to meet-in', Un-cle Joe, Un-cle Joe? Did you ev-er go to meet-in', Un-cle Joe?_____ Did you ev-er go to meet-in', Un-cle Joe, Un-cle Joe? Don't mind the wea-ther when the wind don't blow.

CHORUS

Hop up, my la-dies, three in a row, Hop up, my la-dies, three in a row, Hop up, my la-dies, three in a row, Don't mind the wea-ther when the wind don't blow. wind don't blow.

2. Will your horse carry double, Uncle Joe, Uncle Joe? *etc.*

3. Is your horse a single-footer, Uncle Joe, Uncle Joe? *etc.*

4. Would you rather ride a pacer, Uncle Joe, Uncle Joe? *etc.*

"Uncle Joe" by Alan Lomax. Used by permission of Ludlow Music, Inc., New York.

One of the most important events on the Kentucky frontier was a wedding. Feasting and fun lasted most of the day and night. A party called the "infare" was given by the groom's parents on the following day. This was another all-night celebration. On the third day, when the new couple had moved to their own cabin, they were given a "shivaree" or housewarming. Couples arrived, bringing with them anything that would make a loud noise. They surrounded the cabin, and, at a given signal, there was shouting, gunfire, beating on pans, whistling, and Indian war whoops.

Turnpike Travelers to the Old Northwest

The land north of the Ohio and east of the Mississippi was known as the Northwest Territory after 1787. Early life in the Old Northwest was like that in Kentucky in many ways. The first log cabins were crudely built. Later, log houses took the place of cabins. Many of these houses were two stories high and had narrow corner stairways. Timbers were cut to allow for doors, a fireplace and a chimney. The openings for doors and windows were framed with heavy planks, while the floors were made of wide boards sawed from black walnut logs. Glass for windows came by riverboat from Pennsylvania.

The log house was usually surrounded by other buildings. Horses and cows were stabled in the barn, and corn was stored there in a dry crib. There was a shed for a wagon, with room for a carriage if the family was lucky enough to own one.

The woodshed was near the kitchen door. Many chores were done under its roof. Fat from different kinds of meat was cooked to get grease or lard for making soap. Some butchering of animals for a family meat supply was done under this roof, too.

50

Meat was cured or preserved by smoking it over a slow fire in a shed called the smokehouse. Behind the smokehouse a big hopper, or container, was kept. Into it was poured ashes which accumulated from the fireplace during the winter. From these ashes, lye was produced or "leached" for soap making in the spring.

Wool was carded and spun by the pioneer women and girls of the Old Northwest, just as it was done in Old Kentucky. However, what they didn't knit into stockings, mittens, and scarves, they sent out to be woven into blankets, and the coarse cloth they called "jeans." This cloth took the place of the linsey-woolsey of earlier days. The frontier mother made clothes for her entire family from jeans. Linen was still spun and woven, but cotton from the South was widely used for making sheets and men's shirts.

Near the house the mother and children almost always had a garden. In it they grew greens, melons and root vegetables. Vegetables such as turnips and cabbage were wrapped with straw and buried in the ground for winter use. Potatoes and apples were kept in an earth-floored cellar under the house. Winter squashes and onions were kept in the kitchen where they would stay dry.

The frontier mother did her cooking on the hearth or in the fireplace. Even after stoves were available, some women preferred to cook in the old way, as their mothers before them had done. This photograph of an exhibit in a museum shows many of the household articles that were prized by pioneer mothers. What are some of the things you see that would look strange in a kitchen today?

A Pioneer Kitchen Exhibit

Rock-a-bye Baby

With swinging motion

Rock- a- bye ba - by in the tree - top:

When the wind blows the cra - dle will rock; When the bough bends the

cra - dle will fall, And down will come ba - by, cra - dle and all.

The cradle in the photograph, page 51, is a doll cradle, but full-size cradles were made in the same way. Mothers could rock the cradle with one foot and sing the baby to sleep while sewing or peeling potatoes. This old lullaby was a favorite in pioneer times, as it is today.

As soon as pioneer boys and girls were old enough, they had to do chores to help the family. The boy in this picture is doing one of his daily chores. What is he using to get water for drinking? From the picture, what else might you say about pioneer children?

Library of Congress

In the Old Northwest, certain luxuries could be bought that were not available in Kentucky. Keelboats from Natchez and New Orleans brought sugar and molasses to the settlements. Downriver from Pittsburgh came coffee, chocolate and spices.

Corn bread was still baked, but now wheat bread also could be made from flour that was ground at a nearby mill. The bread was kneaded with home-cultured yeast, left to rise in a covered dough trough, and baked in a stone oven beside the fireplace.

A Corn Husking Bee

For many years, corn was the most important crop in the Old Northwest. At harvest time the farmer invited the neighbors in for a corn-husking bee in his barn. This contest was different from the husking party in Kentucky. Here, girls joined in the fun. The finder of a rare red ear of corn could claim a kiss. If any young man turned up a black ear, his face was smudged with lamp black. Red ear or black, as you can imagine, there was much giggling and teasing.

A corn-husking bee often was the occasion for singing and playing party games, too. One of the most popular was *Shuckin' of the Corn.* The words of this song seem to be saying that a young man has decided to stay close to his true love instead of going to sea on his ship.

Shuckin' of the Corn

1. I have a ship on the o - cean, _____
All lined with sil - ver and gold, _____
Be - fore I'd see my true love suf - fer,
That ship should be an - chored and sold. _____

Refrain
I'm a - go - in' to the shuck - in' of the corn, _____
I'm a - go - in' to the shuck - in' of the corn, _____
A - shuck - in' of the corn and a - blow - in' of the horn,
I'm a go - in' to the shuck - in' of the corn. _____

2. The wind blows cold in Cairo,
The sun refuses to shine,
Before I'd see my true love suffer,
I'd work all the summer time.

The frontier father mended his family's shoes. When shoes were completely beyond repair, a shoemaker in the nearest village made new ones. He used leather from the family's share of the hides that had been taken to the tanner, whose work was almost always paid for with extra leather.

The shoemaker measured the person's feet, whittled a "last" or model out of wood, and then made both shoes the same! The person wearing the shoes interchanged them from day-to-day to make them wear evenly. On the frontier most men wore boots because, in mud or snow, high boots were more practical than low shoes. Sturdy shoes were worn by women on Sundays and throughout the winter months. On summer days, feet were more comfortable without shoes.

Clothes were homemade and very simple. The early pioneers made little attempt to follow fashion. Most Northwest pioneer men never wore buckskin clothing, as men did in Kentucky. Instead, they wore loose trousers, usually tucked into their boot-tops. The homemade coats came below the hips and were worn with scarves and mittens as protection against cold weather. A fur or wool cap with ear flaps was worn in winter; in summer, pioneer farmers wore wide straw hats.

Women, after hearing about the clothes of the ladies of fashion in the Eastern part of the country, made short-waisted dresses. However, they didn't make skirts so tight that they interfered with walking, as did the Eastern ladies. When frontier women and girls went outside, they wore wide-brimmed sunbonnets. These were the same kind that were worn by women moving westward in covered wagons.

Young girls wore shorter copies of their mother's dresses. Sometimes they were very plain, tent-like dresses, with no waist lines. Boys wore pants that reached to the calves of their legs. On Sundays, short jackets were worn with this same kind of pants.

At first in the Old Northwest there were settlements of Virginians, New Englanders, Pennsylvanians, and others. You could tell where people came from by the kind of towns they started and the houses they built. However, in a few years the settlers all became "Westerners." Here, any man was as good as another.

The people of the western frontier were patriotic. Everyone from miles around came into town to celebrate the Fourth of July. Some parents rode on horseback, carrying the babies, while the older children walked. Other families came in wagons. Young men rode their best horses, with their sweethearts riding "pillion" behind them.

The militia held its drill and paraded to the music of fifes and drums. The soldiers fired a volley, which often was followed by cannon fire. What kind of tunes do you think were played for marching? Do you know this tune? It was sung first by the British to the Yankees during the Revolutionary War. Then the Yankees struck up the tune as they marched the defeated British soldiers to prison. This tune was typical of the lively happy-go-lucky spirit of America. People sang and danced to it. On the next page, find dance directions for this song. Sing along with the dance, if you have enough breath!

Yankee Doodle

Fath'r and I went down to camp, A - long with Cap - tain Good' - in,

And there we saw the men and boys As thick as hast - y pud - din'.

REFRAIN

Yan - kee Doo - dle keep it up, Yan - kee Doo - dle dan - dy,

Mind the mu - sic and the step, And with the girls be hand - y.

YANKEE DOODLE
THE DANCE

Form a large triple circle about the room, each "man" having two "ladies", one on each arm. All face and move counter-clockwise.

SING - - - - - - and - - - - - - DANCE

Fath'r and I went down to camp,
Along with Captain Good'in,
And there we saw the men and boys
As thick as hasty puddin'.
Yankee Doodle, keep it up,
Yankee Doodle dandy,

Mind the music and the step,
And with the girls be handy.

All walk forward briskly around the circle — 16 steps. (The check marks over the words tell when to step.)

Each man, dropping the arm of the lady on his L, links R arm with the R lady, and skips about with her twice in a small circle, 8 skips. ("Lonesome ladies" keep time to the music by clapping vigorously.)

Then, without breaking the rhythm or stopping, each man links L arm with the other lady, and skips about twice with her for 8 skips.

Now the men move on to the next two ladies and go through the dance with them. This may be repeated with as many new partners as desired.

"Yankee Doodle" (song and dance directions) from *Sing and Dance* by Beatrice A. Hunt and Harry Robert Wilson. Used by permission of the publishers, Schmitt, Hall and McCreary Company, Minneapolis, Minn.

After the parade was over, people listened to patriotic speeches and ate huge picnic lunches. Almost always there was a great feast of meat. It was roasted over pits by men who had stayed awake all during the previous night to see that it was turned at just the right time.

Some families, returning home early from the parade, celebrated together in their own front yards. How are different members of this family celebrating the Fourth of July?

The Fourth of July

Some people continued the celebration late into the night. Reels and cotillions were danced to fiddle music. Perhaps you would like to learn another of the dances that early Americans enjoyed during the Fourth of July celebration—the Virginia Reel. Try doing this dance to the song, "Turkey in the Straw." You will find it on the next page.

The Virginia Reel

Formation: Girls' row faces boys' row; space between. *Step:* Quiet skip throughout.

Dance: Each number below (1-5) takes one 4-measure phrase in song.
1. Two lines meet in center and return to place.
2. All partners join right hands, go around each other and return to place.
3. Same, using left hands.
4. Same, using both hands.
5. Do-si-do. Partners move forward, passing right shoulders; step across right, back to back, and move backwards into place.

Reel: Head couple slides sideways to foot of line and back, both hands joined. Leaving right hands joined, they go round each other until the girl can grasp the left hand of the 2nd couple boy, while her partner grasps the left hand of the 2nd couple girl. These swing round until the head couple meets in the center, where they again join right hands and swing round until they can join left hands with the 3rd couple. This continues until each has swung all the dancers in the opposite line, after which head couple slides back to place between the lines.

Cast-off: Head girl goes back of girls' line, followed by girls, to position formerly occupied by foot girl. Boys do the same back of boys' line. Head couple, meeting, make arch through which other couples go. Original head couple remains at foot. Dance is repeated with new couple at head.

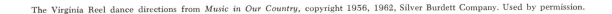

The Virginia Reel dance directions from *Music in Our Country*, copyright 1956, 1962, Silver Burdett Company. Used by permission.

Turkey in the Straw

Briskly

As — I was a-goin' down the road, Tired — team and a heav-y load, Crack my whip and the lead-er sprung; I says day - day — to the wag — on tongue.

Refrain

Tur-key in the straw, tur-key in the straw, Tur-key in the hay, tur-key in the hay, Roll 'em up and twist 'em up a high tuck-a-haw, And — hit 'em up a tune — called — Tur-key in the Straw!

2 Went out to milk and I didn't know how,
I milked the goat instead of the cow.
A monkey sittin' on a pile of straw,
A winkin' at his mother-in-law.

3 Came to the river and I couldn't get across
Paid five dollars for an old blind hoss
Wouldn't go ahead, nor he wouldn't stand still,
So he went up and down like an old saw mill.

"Turkey in the Straw" from *Music in Our Country,* copyright 1956, 1962, Silver Burdett Company. Used by permission.

Camp Meetings

Before churches could be built and a regular minister hired, a kind of traveling minister or preacher followed the early frontier trails and visited one community after another. He was called a "circuit rider." His preaching circuit, or circle, usually took about six weeks to complete, and almost always he preached outdoors. Usually he stayed in one place for several days. People came from miles around to hear him, camping in tents, wagons and lean-tos in the woods around the meeting ground. For this reason, the services came to be called "camp meetings."

The first meeting of this kind was held at Cave Ridge, Kentucky, in 1801. Camp meetings soon became popular both north and south of the Ohio. The circuit riding preacher made his rounds in all kinds of weather and without thought of being paid. He traveled alone on horseback with a Bible, a hymn book, and, if he were lucky, a kind of cape or blanket to keep him warm.

People looked forward to camp meetings for reasons other than to hear the preaching. This was a chance to visit with neighbors and perhaps to hear news from far-away places. Young men might meet girls who were interested in getting married. Contests of different kinds were arranged among the men. Among the many different activities, singing seemed to be one that was enjoyed by everyone. Here is a favorite song of the early camp meetings.

The Saint's Delight

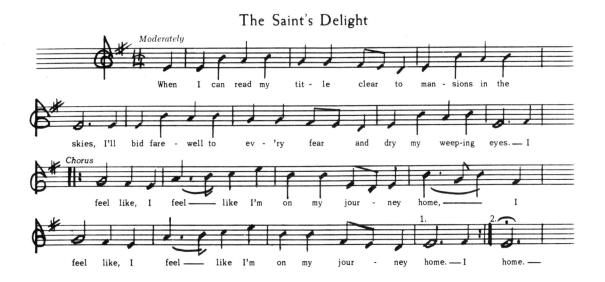

Because roads in the Old Northwest followed along a six-mile square, villages soon grew up at many of the crossroads. But the first villages were on the waterways. Some streams served as roads. Even shallow streams could be made to turn water-wheels. Just downstream from the best spot for a dam, a town might start.

The grist mill or the saw mill became the center around which craftsmen and tradesmen collected to serve the people of the surrounding countryside. Soon the needs of these workers required materials from the East. Men drove oxen, hitched to big wagons, to the nearest large center, perhaps one built on the banks of the Ohio River. They hauled flour, hides, hams and other produce to this center to be sold. Soon the wagons were bringing back glassware, broadcloth, velvet, fiddles, snuff, spectacles, gloves, candlesticks, hats, books and many other things. People had been able to get along without these things, but they were very happy to have a few luxuries once again.

The axe has cut the forest down,
The laboring ox has smoothed all clear,
Apples now grow where pine trees stood,
And slow cows graze instead of deer.

Where Indian fires once raised their smoke
The chimneys of a farm house stand,
And cocks crow barnyard challenges
To dawns that once saw savage land.

The axe, the plow, the binding wall,
By these the wilderness is tamed,
By these the white man's will is wrought,
The rivers bridged, the new towns named.

—Elizabeth Coatsworth

Westward Across the Mississippi

After our government completed the great Louisiana Purchase in 1803, a part of this new land was designated as the Louisiana Territory. All the rest became Missouri.

Missouri pioneers, except for the original French settlers, followed the older patterns of the frontier. Some fathers, it was said, advised their sons to stay at least fifty miles ahead of settlers if they didn't want to be crowded!

Two famous men who took this advice were Kit Carson and Daniel Boone. Boone explored the country before 1800 when it was still owned by Spain. The Spanish gave him a land grant of 8500 acres, and he stayed there with his sons to farm it. Another thing he did was to boil the water from the salt springs of Missouri, and freight the salt down-river in hollow-log boats called pirogues, to sell in St. Louis.

St. Louis was only a small trading center in 1800. But because of its location with reference to the great tradeways, the Ohio, Mississippi and Missouri Rivers, it became known as the Gateway to the West, the "jumping-off" place for western explorers and travelers.

People from Virginia, the Carolinas, Indiana, Ohio, Tennessee and Kentucky kept moving into this new country. By 1850, Kentucky alone had lost 70,000 settlers to Missouri.

One young man, William Stuart, followed the early trails into Missouri on foot. He searched until he found the place where he wanted to build his home. The land was located near the present town of Joplin. After a year of hard work, during which he cleared a field and built a small log cabin, he returned to Kentucky to get his family. Among things the Stuarts took to their new home were some young apple trees. These trees were carried with their roots wrapped in damp soil. Because William Stuart did not trust the packhorses with these precious trees, he carried them on his own back. They were planted near the new home. For many years, the trees grew and produced crops of apples. Why do you think apples were such a treat for people on the frontier? Does this make you think of a certain folklore character who spent his life planting appleseeds? Here is one of the favorite stories of Johnny Appleseed. Although Johnny is a legendary character, he is actually known to have lived. See if there is anything in this story that you find hard to believe.

Johnny Appleseed first arrived in the Ohio Territory around 1801. It was a beautiful land laced with rivers and streams, with great forests and lovely foliage, but in it lived dangerous animals such as wolves, bears, wild hogs and, in places, rattlesnakes.

"Johnny Appleseed" reprinted by permission of Time and Life Books, Inc., from *The Treasury of American Folklore* by the Editors of Time-Life, Inc., copyright 1961.

Johnny saw only the beauty; he seemed to be unaware of the dangers. Sometimes Johnny traveled on horseback. Once in a while he took the river routes in two canoes that were tied together. But most often he traveled on foot. Always he carried a leather sack filled with apple seeds.

Johnny obtained the seeds from the cider mills of western Pennslyvania, to which he repeatedly made trips. He planted the seeds in little patches in the wilderness, selecting the spots partly for their scenic beauty. Johnny believed that fruit was one of God's great gifts to men. He decided that his life's work would be to sow the seeds that would assure plentiful fruit for the pioneers who then were just beginning to turn their faces west. Johnny blazed trails and did his planting well in advance of the wave of settlers.

He did his work with disregard for his own safety and comfort. Usually he went barefoot, despite brambles, stones, stinging insects and snakes. Once a settler, seeing him plodding barefoot through the mud and snow of November, gave him a pair of shoes, only to come upon him a few days later again barefoot. When asked about the shoes, Johnny explained that he had come upon a poor family that needed shoes worse than he. He had given the shoes away.

For many years, Johnny's clothing consisted of castoffs given him by settlers. In later life he wore a coffee sack, with holes cut in it for his head and arms. For something to cover his head, he at one time wore the tin pan he used to cook his food in. Later he was seen wearing a long peaked cap made of pasteboard.

Curiously, Johnny seemed unable to feel pain. When he suffered a sore or cut, he treated it with a red-hot iron. He didn't seem to mind the hurt.

Everyone respected Johnny. Even the Indians never harmed him, because they admired his courage and his ability to endure pain. The settlers loved him for his kindness and humility. Even the boys of the small rough towns never teased Johnny, whose strange appearance might well have made him one of their favorite targets. Little girls adored Johnny because he brought them scraps of ribbon and pieces of calico. He was welcome in any remote cabin where he might stop for a night's lodging. He almost always slept on the floor, and before bedtime he always read aloud either from the New Testament or from the works of Emanuel Swedenborg. As he took out his books, he often said to his listeners, who might be lonely farm people who were hungry for news, "I will read you some news right fresh from heaven."

The Indians did not bother Johnny

even during the War of 1812, when they roved the countryside to burn and kill as allies of the British. Johnny acted as a midwest Paul Revere, warning farmers of the approach of Indian and British raiders, and giving them time to reach the safety of the often distant blockhouses.

Although Johnny never had any possessions, he seldom was completely without money. He charged the settlers who could afford it for his little groves of seedlings. He was a wise planter, locating his nurseries so that the small trees would be ready for transplanting just about the time settlers arrived in the area. However, Johnny spent almost nothing of what he earned on himself, preferring to use his money to help animals.

Johnny could not bear to see any living thing suffer or die. There was no Society for the Prevention of Cruelty to Animals along the advancing frontier, and often a settler's horse or other animal was turned loose to die when it was ailing. Hearing about such cases, Johnny would buy the animal from its owner, nurse it back to health, and then give it to another settler on condition that it be well-treated. Or he would pay for the animal's winter lodging until he could find a good pasture for it in the spring.

Johnny even opposed the pruning or grafting of apple trees, feeling the cuts caused the trees pain. One cold night he put out his campfire because he noticed that it was drawing mosquitoes and that some insects, coming too close

to the flames, were being burned to death. On another occasion, when a hornet got inside his clothes and stung him repeatedly, Johnny removed the insect with care and set it free.

There are many more tales of Johnny's kindness to animals. Once on the trail a rattlesnake fastened its fangs in Johnny's right hand. An Indian who was walking with him struck the snake and killed it. Johnny scolded him sharply.

"The snake didn't go to hurt me," he said. "He didn't know any better."

When Johnny found a wolf caught in a trap and badly hurt, he released it and nursed it. The wolf became a pet and followed Johnny about like a dog until someone shot it.

An old hunter used to tell that he had seen Johnny in the deep wood playing with three bear cubs while the mother bear calmly looked on. Perhaps she was the same creature that he had befriended when, some time before, Johnny had built his campfire one cold night at the end of a hollow log. He intended to crawl into the log for the night, but discovered that a bear and her cubs were already there.

"Poor innocent things," Johnny is said to have remarked. "I am glad I did not turn you out of your house." Then he carefully removed his fire and slept on the snow.

Johnny could endure the very coldest kind of weather. Once he started across Lake Erie with another man, walking barefooted on the ice. Night caught

them in the middle of the lake. The temperature suddenly began to drop, the wind rose, and Johnny's companion froze to death in the bitter cold. Johnny, however, kept warm by rolling over and over on the ice. The next morning he got up and went on across the lake.

Johnny would never touch tea or coffee. He said that when he got to the next world he could not have them and so he did not want to develop a taste for them here. But milk and honey were different. He pointed out that these were heavenly foods. He drank milk whenever he could get it, and he loved honey. There was a great deal of

wild honey in the Ohio woods, but if Johnny found a bee tree, he always looked carefully to see whether the insects had enough for the winter before he touched the comb.

Johnny seldom ate inside a house. He preferred to take his lunch and supper by himself outdoors. Through most of his younger years, he did not bother housewives or landlords with requests for lodging. Who would want to sleep on a cabin floor if he could have, instead, the luxury of a tree-swung hammock? There, as happy as a king, he would sleep, read or sing when resting from his labors.

By the time Johnny was in his early 60's, the areas through which he had traveled and planted so richly—the Ohio River Valley, the lands along the Licking and Muskingum Rivers and White Woman's Creek—were filling up with people. Johnny felt his work was done in that region, so he toured the houses throughout the area and said good-bye to his friends. He then moved west, and for the next nine years he planted in western Ohio and Indiana. One warm evening when he was 72 years old, he appeared at the home of a settler in Allen County, Indiana. Although he was invited to eat with the family, he chose to take some bread and milk and sit on the doorstep where he watched the evening sun go down. Later, having read the Beatitudes aloud, he lay down on the floor to sleep. Next morning he was found, dying and speechless, but in that state of utter peace peculiar to a man who is certain of where he is going next.

Cincinnati Historical Society

Southern Planters Move Westward

During the time that people were leaving Kentucky, some southern people were moving westward, too. More and more cotton was needed by the English textile mills. The use of water power for spinning yarn and weaving cloth had made this industry very profitable. Southern planters now had cotton gins to separate the seed from cotton fiber, and they were anxious to sell cotton to English mills.

But land space for growing cotton was the planter's big problem. Poor farming practices had worn out the soil of many plantations east of the Appalachian Mountains. When cotton is planted year after year in the same field, the soil loses the kinds of plant foods and minerals that are needed to grow good cotton. People had not yet learned about soil conservation through rotation of crops.

Keep in the Middle of the Road

Bracketed passages are all the same.
*Chorus

2. I don't have time to stop and talk,
    Keep in the middle of the road;
    'Cause the road is rough and hard to walk,
    Keep in the middle of the road.
  I fix my eye on the golden stair,
    And I'll keep on going till I get there,
  A golden crown I know I'll wear,
    Keep in the middle of the road.

In search of fertile land, some planters moved their families and slaves over the mountains from Georgia and the Carolinas. They moved into what is now Tennessee, Alabama and Mississippi. They bought some cleared land from people who wanted to keep moving still farther west. Negro workers cleared many more acres. As they worked, they sang to make their work easier.

The large southern landholdings were called plantations. Plantation owners often lived in cities like Mobile or New Orleans. They traveled back and forth to their cotton plantations which were managed by men called "overseers."

Cotton was picked by the Negroes. This was hard work that required bending over and pulling a heavy sack along the cotton rows during the long, hot hours of the day.

Read this poem and try to picture how it would feel to be a cotton picker.

Brown backs bending
Between the cotton rows,
Voices raised in sudden song
"Nobody knows . . ."
Carriage at the Big House,
Visitors from town,
Field hands keep on working
Up the rows and down.
Brown arms slashing
At the tangled cane,
Harnessed mules a-waiting —
"Ain't gonna rain."
Big-hatted planter
Speaking soft and slow;
But all that was very many
Many years ago.   —Anonymous

The Negroes sang as they picked the cotton. Some of their songs described their miseries and expressed their dreams of being released from slavery. *Michael, Row the Boat Ashore* was such a song.

Michael, Row the Boat Ashore

Slowly

Hal - le - lu - jah,　Hal - le - lu - jah.

Broadly

1. Mi - chael, row the boat a - shore, Hal - le - lu - jah! Mi - chael, row the boat a -

shore, Hal - le - lu - jah! Mi - chael boat a gos - pel boat, Hal - le -

lu - jah! Mi - chael boat a gos-pel boat, Hal - le - lu - jah!

2. Michael boat a music boat, Hallelujah!
   Michael boat a music boat, Hallelujah!
   Gabriel, blow the trumpet horn, Hallelujah!
   Gabriel, blow the trumpet horn, Hallelujah!

3. Brother, lend a helpin' hand, Hallelujah!
   Brother, lend a helpin' hand, Hallelujah!
   Boastn' talk will sink your soul, Hallelujah!
   Boastn' talk will sink your soul, Hallelujah!

4. Jordan stream is wide and deep, Hallelujah!
   Jordan stream is wide and deep, Hallelujah!
   Jesus stand on t'other side, Hallelujah!
   Jesus stand on t'other side, Hallelujah!

The big bales of cotton were loaded aboard the river boats for the trip down-river to market. As the Negroes worked at the task, they sang. One acted as the lead singer. He started a song and others joined in. They worked to the rhythm of the song. As you might suspect, songs sung in this way were called work songs. Read the words of this song. Could it have been a work song?

While Negroes as slaves in the New World lost their African tribal languages and some of their tribal customs, they kept certain of their folk tales. Among these were the animal stories that were told and retold, usually to entertain children. Some of these stories were actually about personal experiences and hopes. In African animal stories, the heroes were generally the jackal, the hare and the tortoise. In America, the jackal was represented by the fox, the African hare by the rabbit, and the tortoise by the dry-land turtle or terrapin. As a villain, the African hyena was replaced by the wolf, bear or fox. Animal characters such as lions, leopards, tigers and monkeys were not replaced, however. Can you guess why?

"Michael, Row the Boat Ashore" from *22 Favorite Folk Songs*, published by The Richmond Organization, New York.

Pick a Bale of Cotton

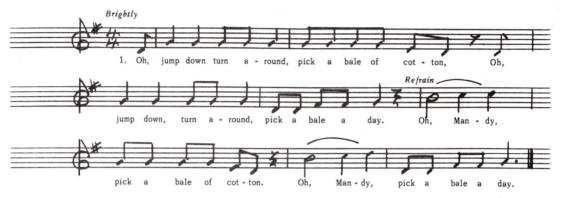

1. Oh, jump down turn a-round, pick a bale of cot-ton, Oh, jump down, turn a-round, pick a bale a day. Oh, Man-dy, pick a bale of cot-ton. Oh, Man-dy, pick a bale a day.

2. Oh, me and my partner can —
3. Me and my wife can —
4. Had a little woman could —

5. I b'lieve to my soul I can —
6. Went to Corsicana to —

The American Negro slave, adopting Br'er Rabbit as a story hero, described him as the most frightened and helpless of creatures. But they gave him other qualities as well. He was a practical joker, a braggart, a wit, a glutton, a lady's man and a trickster. His most important quality was the ability to get the best of bigger and stronger animals. In this story, recorded by Joel Chandler Harris, how did Br'er Rabbit get the best of Br'er Fox?

Uncle Remus Initiates The Little Boy
by
Joel Chandler Harris

One evening recently, the lady whom Uncle Remus calls "Miss Sally" missed her little seven-year-old. Making search for him through the house and through the yard, she heard the sound of voices in the old man's cabin, and, looking, through the window, saw the child sitting by Uncle Remus. His head rested against the old man's arm, and he was gazing with an expression of the most intense interest into the rough, weather-beaten face that beamed so kindly upon him. This is what Miss Sally heard:

Bimeby, one day, after Br'er Fox bin doin' all dat he could fer ter ketch Br'er Rabbit, en Br'er Rabbit bin doin' all he could fer ter keep 'im fum it, Br'er Fox say to hisse'f dat he'd put up a game on Br'er Rabbit, en he ain't mo'n got de wuds out'n his mouf twel Br'er Rabbit, sezee, sorter mendin' his road, lookin' des ez plump, en ez fat, en ez sassy ez a Moggin hoss in a barley-patch.

"Hol' on dar, Br'er Rabbit," sez Br'er Fox, sezee.

"I ain't got time, Bre'er Fox," sez Br'er Rabbit, sezee, sorter mendin' his licks.

"I wanter have some confab wid you, Br'er Rabbit," sez Br'er Fox, sezee.

"All right, Br'er Fox, but you better holler fum whar you stan'. I'm monstus full er fleas dis mawnin'," sez Br'er Rabbit, sezee.

"I seed Br'er B'ar yistiddy," sez Br'er Fox, sezee, "en he sorter rake me over de coals kaze you en me ain't make frens en live naberly, en I tole 'im dat I'd see you."

Den Br'er Rabbit scratch one year wid his off hinefoot sorter jub'usly, en den he ups en sez, sezee:

"All a settin', Br'er Fox. Spose'n you drap roun' temorrer en take dinner wid me. We ain't got no great doin's at our house, but I speck de ole' woman en de chilluns kin sorter scramble roun' en git up sump'n fer ter stay yo' stummuck."

"I'm 'gree'ble, Br'er Rabbit," sez Br'er Fox, sezee.

"Den I'll 'pen' on you," sez Br'er Rabbit, sezee.

Nex' day, Mr. Rabbit an' Mizz Rabbit got up soon, 'fo' day, en raided on a gyarden like Miss Sally's out dar, en got some cabbiges, en some roas'n years, en some sparrer-grass, en day fix up a smashin' dinner. Bimeby one er de little Rabbits, playin' out in the back-yard, come runnin' in hollerin', "Oh, ma! oh, ma! I seed Mr. Fox a comin'!" En den Br'er Rabbit he tuck de chilluns by der years en make um set down, en den him en Mizz Rabbit sorten dally roun' waitin' for Br'er Fox. En day keep on waitin', but no Br'er Fox ain't come. Atter' while Br'er Rabbit goes to de do', easy like, en peep out, en dar, stickin' out fum behime de cornder, wuz de

tip-een' er Br'er Fox tail. Den Br'er Rabbit shut de do' en sot down, en put his paws behime his years en begin fer ter sing:

"De place wharbouts you spill de grease,
    Right dar youer boun' ter slide,
An' whar you fine a bunch er ha'r,
    You'll sholy fine de hide."

Nex' day, Br'er Fox sent word by Mr. Mink, en skuze hisse'f kaze he wuz too sick fer ter come, en he ax Br'er Rabbit fer ter come en take dinner wid him, en Br'er Rabbit say we wuz 'gree'ble.

Bimeby, we'n de shadders wuz at der shortes', Br'er Rabbit he sorter brush up en santer down ter Br'er Fox's house, en w'en he got dar, he hear somebody groanin', en he look in de do' e dar he see Br'er Fox settin' up in a rockin' cheer all wrop up wid flannil, en he look mighty weak. Br'er Rabbit look all 'roun', he did, but he ain't see no dinner. De dishpan wuz settin' on de table, en close by wuz a kyarvin' knife.

"Look like you gwineter have chicken fer dinner, Br'er Fox," sez Br'er Rabbit, sezee.

"Yes, Br'er Rabbit, deyer nice, en fresh, en tender," sez Br'er Fox, sezee.

Den Br'er Rabbit sorter pull his mustarsh, en say: "You ain't got no calamus root, is you, Br'er Fox? I done got so now dat I can't eat no chicken 'ceppin she's seasoned up wid calamus root." En wid dat Br'er Rabbit lipt out er de do' and dodge 'mong de bushes, en sot dar watchin' fer Br'er Fox; en he ain't watch long, nudder, kaze Br'er Fox flung off de flannil en crope out er de house en got what he could close in on Br'er Rabbit, en bimeby Br'er Rabbit holler out: "Oh, Br'er Fox! I'll des put yo' calamus root out yer on dish yer stump. Better come git it while hit's fresh." And wid dat Br'er Rabbit gallop off home. En Br'er Fox ain't ketch 'im yit, en w'at's mo', honey, he ain't gwineter.

Can you think of some reasons why Negro slaves seemed to want the smaller animal characters in their folk tales to get the best of the bigger and stronger animals? Perhaps you would like to read some other Negro folk tales. Stories of great exaggeration, describing almost everything, were favorites among the Negro people. Here is a folk tale that teaches a lesson. Can you discover what it is?

Little Eight John

Once long ago there was a little black boy named Eight John. He was a nice looking little boy but he didn't act like he looked. He was a mean little boy an' he wouldn't mind a word the grown folks told him—no, not a livin' word. So if his loving mammy told him not to do a thing, he went straight an' did it.

"Don't step on any toad frogs," his loving mammy told him, "or you will bring bad luck on your family. Yes, you will."

Little Eight John said, "No'm, I won't step on any toad frogs. No ma'am!"

But just as sure as anything, soon as he got out of sight of his loving mammy, that Little Eight John found a toad frog and squashed it. Sometimes he squashed a heap of toad frogs.

Then the cow wouldn't give any good milk and the baby would have the bad old colic.

But Little Eight John just ducked his head and laughed.

"Don't sit in any chair backwards," his loving mammy told Little Eight John. "It will bring weary troubles to your family."

An' so Little Eight John sat backwards in every chair.

Then his loving mammy's cornbread burned and the cream wouldn't churn.

Little Eight John just laughed and laughed and laughed because he knew why this was.

"Don't climb any trees on Sunday," his loving mammy told him, "or it will be bad luck."

So that Little Eight John, that bad little boy, he sneaked up trees on Sunday.

Then his pappy's potatoes wouldn't grow and the mule wouldn't go.

Little Eight John, he knew why.

"Don't count your teeth," his loving mammy told Little Eight John, "or there will be a sad sickness in your family."

But that Little Eight John, he went right ahead an' counted his teeth. He counted his uppers an' he counted his lowers. He counted them on weekdays and on Sundays.

Then his mammy got a cough and the baby got the croup. This was account of that Little Eight John and the badness of a little boy.

"Don't sleep with your head at the foot of the bed or your family will get the weary money blues," his loving mammy told him.

So he did it and did it more, that cross-going Little Eight John boy.

And the family went broke with no money in the poke.

Little Eight John just giggled.

"Don't have any Sunday moans, for fear of Old Raw Head Bloddy Bones," his loving mammy told him.

So he had Sundays moans and he had more Sunday groans, and he moaned and he groaned and he moaned.

And Old Raw Head Bloddy Bones came after that little bad boy and changed him to a little old grease spot on the kitchen table, an' his loving mammy washed it off the next morning.

And that was the end of Little Eight John.

And that is what always happens to never-minding little boys.

Have you heard any of these playsongs and games? Did you know that children are still saying some of the rhymes and playing some of the games that Negro children enjoyed long ago?

Hide and Seek

I got up about half-past four,
Forty-four robbers was 'round my door.
I opened the door and let 'em in,
Hit 'em over the head with a rollin' pin.
All hid? All hid?

Counting Out Rhymes

Out goes the rat.
Out goes the cat.
Out goes the lady with the see-saw hat.
O-U-T spells out and out goes you.

Shoo-Fly, Don't Bother Me

Shoo, shoo, shoo, shoo-fly don't bother me.
Shoo, shoo, shoo, shoo-fly don't bother me.
Oh, shoo-fly, don't bother me,
Shoo-fly, don't bother me,
Shoo-fly, don't bother me,
I belong to the bumblebee.

(Children go around in a circle keeping time to the music. On last four lines, the group stands still and clap hands in time to the song.)

Little David

Lively, Playfully

Lit - tle Da - vid, play on yo' harp, Hal - le - lu! Hal - le - lu!

Lit - tle Da - vid, play on yo' harp, Hal - le lu! Lit - tle Da - vid

play on yo' harp, Hal - le - lu! Hal - le - lu! Lit - tle Da - vid,

Fine

play on yo' harp, Hal - le - lu! Da - vid was a shep - herd boy —

— He killed Go - li - ath and shou - ted for joy. — Lit - tle Da - vid,

Negro Folk Songs

Long before the Civil War, the Negro was singing of freedom. At first, it was freedom as symbolized in religion. Some of the finest spirituals were from the great cotton plantations. One of the most familiar of these is *Little David*.

Plantation owners, observing that their Negro workers were more cheerful and did their tasks better when they sang, encouraged them to sing such songs as *Rock About My Saro Jane.*

Rock About, My Saro Jane

Rowdy

I've got a wife an'-a five l'il' chil - lun, Be - lieve I'll take a trip on the big Mac - Mil - lan, O Sa - ro Jane!

Chorus

O there's noth - ing to do but to sit down an' sing An' rock a - bout, my Sa - ro Jane. O

rock a - bout, my Sa - ro Jane, Rock a - bout, my Sa - ro Jane.

Travelers in the South, before the Civil War, were deeply impressed by the chanting of Negroes as they rowed or paddled in the Louisiana bayous. The Negro axeman, chopping timber to clear the land, chanted . . .

When I was young and in my prime, (hah!)
Sunk my axe deep every time, (hah!)
Now I'm old and my heart's growing cold,
     (hah!)
Can't swing my axe to save my soul. (hah!)
     Come on, Mister Tree, you almost
          down, (hah!)
     Come on, Mister Tree, want to see you
          hit the ground. (hah!)

                    —Anonymous

Much of the land of the South was cleared, plowed, and harvested by Negro workers who sang as they worked. Not many of the songs sung by these people have been preserved. But here is one about Uncle Bob who was married to a woman named Sylvie. As you read the verses, think of the story they tell about these two people. As you sing this song, try to make it sound the way the Negro people may have sung it.

Bring Me Li'l' Water, Sylvie

This man was in the field ploughin' in the two hottest months of the year, which is July and August. He called his wife, Sylvie, the first time and she didn't hear him, so he called her again, a little louder.

> Bring me li'l' water, Sylvie,
> Bring me li'l' water now,
> Bring me li'l' water, Sylvie,
> Ev'ry li'l' once in a while.

That second time Sylvie heard him. She grab her bucket and fill it with cool water from the well, and she went runnin'. Down through the field, the little bucket knockin' against her legs and a little water spillin' out on the cotton dress she wore. She holler back at him to let him know she comin' . . .

> Don't you see me comin'?
> Don't you see me now?
> Don't you see me comin'?
> Ev'ry li'l' once in a while?

It was hot down there and when that man look up and saw li'l' Sylvie comin' trottin' along, he begin to feel good. He commenced to blowin' his horn . . .

> Bring me li'l' water, Sylvie,
> Bring me li'l' water now,
> Bring me li'l' water, Sylvie,
> Ev'ry li'l' once in a while.

Sylvie was just skippin' long now, and when she got up near her husban' she hollered again to show him how glad she was to see him . . .

> Don't you hear me comin'?
> Don't you hear me now?
> Don't you hear me comin'?
> Ev'ry li'l' once in a while.

Well, the man he retch for that bucket and he dip in the dipper an' have him a big, long draught of that cool, well-water, look like it do him good right down to his toes. Sylvie just laugh to see him satisfied. Then he tol' her, 'Now, look here, I'm burnin' down here in this bottom, and when I wants my water I wants you to come in a hurry. So you listen next time when I holler.'

> Bring me li'l' water, Sylvie,
> Bring me li'l' water now,
> Bring me li'l' water, Sylvie,
> Ev'ry li'l' once in a while.
>
> Lawd, Lawd, Sylvie,
> Lawd, Lawd, now!
> Lawd, Lawd, Sylvie,
> Ev'ry li'l' once in a while.

"Bring Me Li'l Water, Sylvie" from *Negro Folk Songs as sung by Leadbelly*, Folkways Music Publishers, Inc.

In Africa, dancing was a natural part of human life. When Negro people were brought to America, however, dancing was still considered something of a sin by many white people. But they watched with pleasure as the Negroes expressed themselves in joyful dances.

As the frontier moved westward, Negroes learned the country dances of the pioneers, the jigging steps, and the old ring game. Even today at many rural schools in the South little girls can be seen playing some of these old ring games at recess. Clapping and chanting in a ring or circle, while in the center of the circle a couple "cut up shines," they move so lightly and gracefully that they seem not to even touch the ground. Here are the words to a ring game from long ago. Do you recognize these words?

Here we go loop de loo,
Here we go loop de loo,
Here we go loop de loo,
All on a Saturday night.

I put my right hand in,
I take my right hand out,
I give my right hand a
shake, shake, shake,
And turn my body about.

I put my left hand in, etc.
I put my right foot in, etc.
I put my left foot in, etc.
I put my big head in, etc.
I put my big self in, etc.

The Northern Frontier

Most people who moved west from New England and New York were not adventurers or hunters like Daniel Boone and Davy Crockett. New England's rocky soil and severe climate had developed habits of thrift and diligence in its settlers, so that when they "went west" they were likely to go as farmers or businessmen.

Most of them resettled in the Great Lakes area and in Michigan Territory. There was not so much mixing of people from different parts of the country here, as there was in Ohio, Indiana, Illinois and Missouri. Except for the old French fur-trading people, Michigan Territory was settled almost entirely by folks from New England and New York.

With the opening of the Erie Canal in 1825, trade between the North Atlantic states and the Great Lakes region increased enormously. The Chicago Road across Michigan gave farmers another way to get their products to market, and it opened still another route to the West for restless pioneers.

Some of the small-town tradesmen of New England became roving merchants, or peddlers. On the frontier they traveled from home to home, particularly in areas where there were no established stores. Leading a pack horse or two, loaded with pots and pans, needles and knives, they were willing to trade for almost anything the housewife had to offer. If the peddler was fortunate enough to have a wagon, it was a special kind built with many compartments to hold different kinds of articles to sell. Traveling alone, he whistled or sang as his horses jogged along. He seemed unconcerned about unfriendly Indians and wild animals.

He came on muleback, dodging Indians as he went, with a pack full of better living and a tongue full of charms...for he was the great American salesman, and no man ever had a better thing to sell. He came by rickety wagon, one jump behind the pioneers, carrying axes for the farmer, fancy dress goods for his wife, and encyclopedias for the farmer's ambitious boy. He was the great practical democrat, spreader of good things among more and more people.

The peddler's arrival at a frontier home was a pleasant event. People without close neighbors welcomed someone to whom they could talk. The peddler brought news from other places. Often he spent the night and was treated as an important guest. He was certain to try to sell or trade the housewife a clock, because this was his specialty. Many other items were brought forth from his pack or wagon: calico, cotton check and gingham cloth from the textile mills of New England, tin cups and plates, iron spoons, coffee pots, thread, pins, horn buttons, shaving soap, ribbon, pepper boxes, sausage stuffers, tablecloths, knives and forks, razors, neckcloths, hose, jew's harp, nutmeg, wax dolls, and New England-made shoes. It is said that some peddlers even sold coffins. On page 86 is a favorite story told about peddlers:

A Yankee peddler with his cart, overtaking another of his kind on the road, was thus addressed: "Hello', what do you carry?"

"Drugs and medicines," was the reply.

"Good," returned the other, "you may go ahead; I carry grave-stones."

A traveling patent-medicine peddler would sing *Doctor Ironbeard* to advertise his wares. One or more instrumentalists might travel with him to attract attention.

Doctor Ironbeard

Oh, I am Doc - tor I - ron - beard, Twi - li wil - li witt, boom boom! I'll

cure your ills with heal - ing art, Twil - li wil - li witt, boom boom! Now

I can make the dumb to walk, Twi - li wil - li witt, boom boom boomboom! The

lame to see, the blind to talk, Twi - li wil - li witt, boom boom! Sing

tor - i - ay, sing tor - i - ay! Twi - li wil - li witt, boom boom boom boom! Sing

tor - i - ay, sing tor - i - ay! Twi - li wil - li witt, boom boom!

When frontiers were settled and trading centers built, the Yankee peddler was no longer needed. In his place was the general storekeeper. The nature of the general store made it a social center. Along with the village tavern, the store served as a gathering place for village loafers, gossips, jesters and story-tellers. Here people met in a daily contest of wit and humor. Here is a sample of the stories they told:

Two men met on the street one day.

One asked, "How do you manage to feed your large family with your small income?"

"Well," the other responded, "I'll tell you. I find out what they don't like and give 'em plenty of it."

Storekeepers sometimes advertised with printed rhymes. After you have read the following advertising rhymes, perhaps you can write others. Remember to advertise items that were for sale in a pioneer store.

Shirts, frocks, shoes, mittens, also hose
And many other kinds of clothes.

Tubs, buckets, pails, and pudding pans
Bandanas, handkerchiefs, and fans.

Books on such subjects as you'll find
A proper food to feast the mind.

The Circus Goes West, Too

One of the greatest wits who ever came out of a pioneer general store was Phineas T. Barnum. As a clerk in his father's store, he learned sharp trades and tricks. Later, as the great circus pioneer, P. T. Barnum developed a kind of advertising that was copied by many businesses and industries. His advertising was very successful. He moved his show to all parts of the western frontier. What does the advertisement above tell you about the circus acts?

Circuses began in America in 1792. They grew and traveled westward as the frontiers moved ahead. The early circuses traveled in wagons pulled by horses over turnpikes or roads that were rough and often muddy. A hippopotamus wagon needed fourteen horses to move it over the poor roads!

There were no railroad circus cars until 1872. Such cars were first used to move the Barnum Circus. Later this circus developed into the Barnum and Bailey Circus, the largest in the United States. A strong rival to this group was the Ringling Brothers Circus. Eventually, Ringling Brothers bought the Barnum and Bailey Show.

A Circus Train

Today we don't have circus parades down the streets of our busy cities. It is just too bad! The parade was almost more exciting than the show itself. A steam calliope, as well as the band, played gay tunes. The red-and-gold wagons, clowns and acrobats, decorated horses, camels and elephants were something a boy or girl could never forget. And the big rumbling calliope, shooting out steam, made the best music in the world! Perhaps you can find a picture of a calliope. How do you think it worked?

Study the picture below. What do you think happened at the first county fairs?

A County Fair

A circus was an important event in a frontier community. Families came from miles around to see it. Usually school was closed so the children could go. Sometimes boys "got in free" by helping to feed and water the animals.

Have you read the story, *Toby Tyler?* Did you discover why Toby ran away from home? Can you picture an early-day circus being moved over a dusty or muddy turnpike in wagons? How do you think lions, tigers, elephants and other animals were loaded or unloaded?

Great Lakes Frontier and Paul Bunyan

The need for lumber in our fast growing country was prodigious. It seemed that we just couldn't get enough. On the frontier thousands of new towns were being built, and in Atlantic shipyards huge fleets of wooden ships were sliding down the ways. New Englanders cut down their own trees, then went west into the Great Lakes region to work at cutting down the great pine forests there.

When a man faced the hardships and dangers of the dark woods of the wintery North it was good to have someone to joke about, and to tell tall tales about. The legend of Paul Bunyan probably grew out of the lies and boasts that were told for amusement during the long, lonely evenings in lumber camps. Paul became the mythical hero of these early lumberjacks. Just as the knights of old had their magic steeds or horses, Paul Bunyan had his giant blue ox, Babe.

Babe could haul a whole forest of logs with a harness of buckskin, which stretched when wet and shrank when dry. On a rainy day, Babe would start hauling his load and arrive in camp by noon, only to find that the stretching buckskin had left the load back in the forest. Then as the sun came out and dried the harness, its shrinking action pulled the load into camp.

Paul Bunyan, with Babe, the blue ox, became the center of many imaginative and poetic exaggerations, probably more than were ever told about any other American legendary hero. In Minnesota, prizes were awarded every year to those who contributed the best tale about Paul Bunyan. One of the prize-winning yarns was about Paul's experience when he went East to try his hand at throwing a dollar across the Potomac River as George Washington had done. The story goes like this:

One day Paul Bunyan was strolling through the North Woods, followed by his faithful blue ox, Babe. Paul had a wanderlust. A tourist had told him the story of how George Washington had thrown a dollar across the Potomac. Paul allowed as how he'd like to take a crack at this game himself. Packing himself a small lunch of five roasted pigs, twenty-five ducks, and forty bushels of rice, Paul headed East. He wasn't sure he'd know the Potomac, but decided he'd keep his eye open for the biggest river in the East. When he finally saw a great expanse of water, he was sure it was the Potomac. He didn't have a dollar, but he found a farmer's wagon and removed the four wheels. To his embarrassment the first two wheels landed in the water, but on the last two tries there was no splash of water—only a cloud of dust as they landed on the opposite shore.

And so, to this day, two farmers in a coastal village in France talk about how a couple of wagon wheels suddenly descended upon them out of the sky. Paul Bunyan never knew that he had mistaken the Atlantic Ocean for the Potomac River.

Some of the stories in the North woods were called "hot stove" tales. After you have read this story, try to make your own hot stove tale.

Benny and the Hot Stove

Benny, the little blue ox of Paul Bunyan, grew two feet every time Paul looked at him. The barn was gone one morning and they found it on Benny's back; he grew right out of it during the night.

One night he kept pawing and bellowing for more pancakes, until there were two hundred men at the cook shanty stove—trying to keep him fed. About breakfast time, Benny broke loose, tore down the cook shanty, and ate all the pancakes that were piled up for the loggers' breakfast. Then Benny made his big mistake; he ate the red hot stove, and that finished him.

"Benny and the Hot Stove" adapted from *A Treasury of American Folklore*, edited by B. A. Botkin. New York: Crown Publishers, Inc.

It was said that only if your heart was made of iron, your soul wrapped in steel, and your skin too tough for bedbug bites—only if you could work up to your waist in snow for a whole winter on starvation wages—were you fit to be a lumberjack. The great lumber camps required an endless supply of such men. They kept coming into the woods—Scots, Swedes, Irish and Yankees. Many of their songs reflected abuses and hardships endured as lumbermen, but these men sang with a lusty joy for life.

Try to imagine a group of lumberjacks singing this alphabet song. What phrases or words help you to know how they felt and lived?

Lumberman's Alphabet

1. A is for Ax, and that we all know, And B is for Boy that can use it also; C is for Chopping we first do begin, And D is for Danger we often fall in.

Refrain

So merry, so merry are we, No mortals on earth are as happy as we. To me I derry O derry I derry down, Use shanty boys well and there's nothing goes wrong.

2. E is for Echo that through the woods rang,
And F is for Foreman, the head of our gang;
G is for Grindstone at night we do turn,
And H is for Handle so smoothly worn.

3. I is for Iron which we mark our pine,
And J is for Jovial we're always inclin';
K is for Keen Edges our axes we keep,
And L is for Lice that keeps us from sleep.

4. M is for Moss which we chink our camp,
And N is for Needle with which we mend our pants;
O is for Owl which hooted at night,
And P is for Pine which we always fall right.

5. Q is for Quickness we put ourselves to,
R is for River we haul the logs to;
S is for Sleds we haul the logs on,
T is for Team that pulls them along.

6. U is for Uses we put ourselves to,
And V is for Valley we haul the logs through;
And W is for Woods we leave in the spring,
And now I have sung all I'm going to sing.

7. X is for Christmas when the yarding's all done,
Y is for Yonder, the set of the sun;
Z is for Zero, in the cold winter time,
And now I have brought all these letters in rhyme.

Turnpike Era Activities

1. Suppose that you were with Daniel Boone when he started out in 1769 to find the trail that led to Kentucky. Use your imagination, along with what you have read. Tell some of the experiences you and the rest of the men had on that exploration trip.

2. Pretend that you are a pioneer living in "Ol' Kaintuck." Pantomime for the class a frightening kind of experience that you had while hunting with your dogs one day.

3. Find out more about how to card wool and spin it into yarn. Try to show the class just how it is done.

4. Get a book from the library that explains how simple looms are made. Make a loom and demonstrate how it works.

5. Try to borrow an old-fashioned churn and show the class how butter was made by the pioneers.

6. Select as a topic, "Early American Inns." Find information and pictures to describe them.

7. Locate some examples of toll roads that are still functioning today. Describe the way toll fees are collected.

8. Plan a "play-party." Ask everyone to dress-up in pioneer costumes. Play the games the way you think they were played at pioneer parties.

9. Build models of covered wagons. Explain the difference between the Conestoga wagons and those used on the Western trails.

10. Do a research project on stagecoaches. Include some of the exciting experiences of stage-coach drivers and passengers.

11. Draw pictures of some of the "fun" times in the life of an early pioneer.

12. Select Daniel Boone as a topic. Make a model of the fort that was named for him.

13. Make a model of a pioneer cabin. Include the things that were kept outside the cabin.

14. Design and make a water wheel. Demonstrate its use for the class.

15. Read additional folk tales about Daniel Boone, Davy Crockett, Paul Bunyan, Uncle Remus and others.

CHAPTER II
WESTWARD BY WATER

94

Traveling Westward on America's Waterways

The Indians were the first to depend on water for transportation in America. Since they traveled by water, they almost always lived near water—rivers, streams or lakes. And since water was so important to them, they made up legends to explain how water came to be where it was. Two of these legends explain the presence of the Finger Lakes in New York and of the Wisconsin River in Wisconsin.

The Finger Lakes of New York

Many, many moons ago there lived a giant in the country around the Great Lakes. He roamed the countryside searching for water. The land was flat and his eye could see great distances, but he could see no water. He decided to make some low places where he could get water. By spreading his fingers wide and pressing them hard against the ground, he made hollow places. The rain filled these hollows with water. They are still full of water today. We call them the Finger Lakes.

Legend of the Wisconsin River

Long, long ago an enormous serpent lived in the Mississippi River. He was anxious to visit the Great Lakes. He was sure it would take too long to go all around by means of the waterways, so he went across land to Green Bay on Lake Michigan. Rolling, winding and twisting, as serpents do, he crawled slowly toward the Great Lakes. His huge body made long hollows in the ground. Gradually these hollows filled with water and became a river. This river is called the Wisconsin River. The trip to the Great Lakes was hard work. When the serpent coiled up and stopped to rest he caused other hollows. These soon filled with water and became the lakes of Wisconsin.

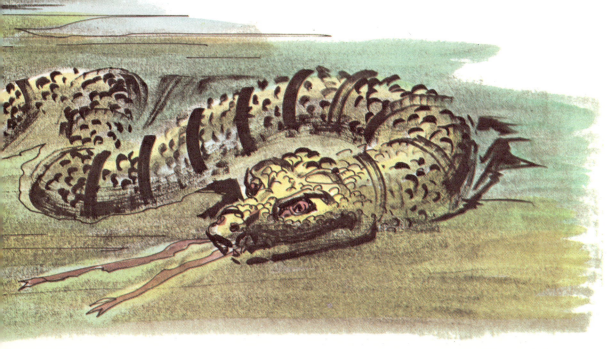

Try creating your own legends. You might create a legend about the birth of the Mississippi River. What kind of legend might you write about the creation of the Gulf of Mexico? The Appalachian Mountains? The high tides of the Maine coast?

As the Indians paddled their canoes along rivers and streams they might have sung this song. Perhaps it helped them to paddle with a rhythm that moved their canoes swiftly through the water.

As you sing, think about the motions of paddling a canoe. After you have learned the song well, sing it as a two-part round.

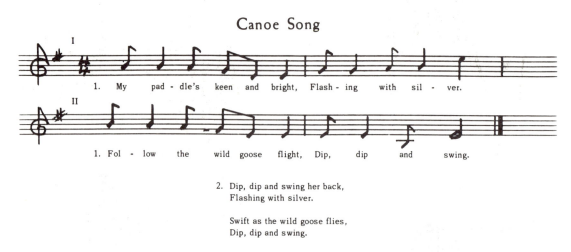

Canoe Song

1. My pad-dle's keen and bright, Flash-ing with sil-ver.

1. Fol-low the wild goose flight, Dip, dip and swing.

2. Dip, dip and swing her back,
   Flashing with silver.

   Swift as the wild goose flies,
   Dip, dip and swing.

"Canoe Song" used by permission of Lynn Rohrbough, Cooperative Recreation Service, Inc., Delaware, Ohio.

The canoe was the simplest and easiest river craft to use in pre-steamboat days. Indians taught the earliest French settlers how to hollow out logs and make canoes. Soon the French were paddling along most of our Northeastern rivers. These hardy adventurers learned from the Indians that inland forests were the homes of numerous fur-bearing animals. With hired Indian guides, trappers explored the Missouri and Mississippi Rivers, and other rivers in Wisconsin and Minnesota.

The rivers were roads for these early Frenchmen who became known as *voyageurs,* or travelers. They were trappers and traders, but later they acted as guides for settlers who ventured into the dense forest lands.

The voyageurs sang continually as they paddled. They sang to keep the paddling rhythm and also to fill the silence. Most of their songs were old folk tunes which came with them from France.

A favorite paddling song of the voyageurs was *En Roulant Ma Boule,* which means "Roll on, my ball." As they paddled along, the travelers made up new verses for the song. They were too busy paddling to add serious verses, so to fill in the words they would simply repeat the phrase, "Roll on, my ball." Can you add more verses to this song?

En Roulant Ma Boule

2. And ducks play on it all day long,
   They swim and float and sing this song.

3. They swim and float and sing this song,
   One day a hunter came along.

4. One day a hunter came along,
   And saw those ducks upon the pond.

5. He saw those ducks upon the pond,
   And scared them so that up they bound.

6. He scared them so that up they bound,
   Their fluffy feathers drifting down.

7. Their fluffy feathers drifting down,
   Down, down, down upon the ground.

Words for "En Roulant Ma Boule" from *More Songs To Grow On* by Beatrice Landeck, published by Edward B. Marks Music Corporation. Music from *Music In Our Country,* Book 5, Silver Burdett Company. Both used by permission.

The song *Alouette* was a favorite of all French settlers. Study the words carefully. Try to find someone who speaks French to help you with the pronunciation of these French words.

"Gentil Alouette" means "pretty meadow lark." "Je te plumerai" means "I shall pick off your feathers." The words "la tete" mean head, "le bec" means beak, "le cou" means neck, "le dos" means back; and "les pattes" means feet.

Alouette is an action song. As you sing it, touch the part of your body that you are singing about. Sing the song in a "conversation" style. It is fun to pick a leader to sing the leader's part and to have the rest of the group sing the chorus.

Alouette

Lively

Chorus
A - lou - et - te, gen - til A - lou - et - te, A - lou - et - te, Je te plu - me - rai. *Fine*

Leader
1. Je te plu - me - rai la tête, **Chorus** Je te plu - me - rai la tête,

Leader Et la tête, et la tête, **Chorus** **Leader** A - lou - ette, **Chorus** A - lou - ette, O! *D.C. al fine*

2. Je te plu - me - rai la bec, Je te plu - me - rai la bec,
Et le bec, et le bec, Et la tete, et la tete,

In this action song, when you sing "la tête" touch your head; when you sing "le bec" touch your nose; when you sing "le cou" touch your neck; when you sing "le dos" touch your back; when you sing "les pattes" touch your feet.

After the first stanza, repeat the measure between the repeat bars with the words in reverse order. For example, the last stanza is: Et les pattes, et les pattes; Et le dos, et le dos; Et le cou, et le cou; Et le bec, et le bec; Et la tète, et la tète, Alouette, Alouette, O!

The canoe was the chief means of transportation for both the Indians and the French voyageurs. Years later the canoe was equally important to other trappers, traders, peddlers, settlers, explorers, adventurers, map makers and military men.

Wagons Westward

We have seen how trail breakers into the "wild West" were followed by home-steaders who brought families, tools, livestock and seeds for the first sowing. After the French and Spanish had given up their western holdings, and particularly after the Louisiana Purchase in 1803, Americans in still greater numbers were eager to push the frontier farther west.

But travel in the mud and ruts of the overland routes, as we have seen, was slow and arduous work. Whenever they could, travelers took advantage of the "nat-ural highways," the navigable creeks, rivers and lakes. By 1800 the canoe, barge, keelboat and flatboat were in wide use on the Ohio, Tennessee, Missouri and Mississippi Rivers.

To the pioneer traveler, "the promised land" meant not only the Heavens above, but the rich, fertile soil on the other side of the Alleghenies, and the land stretching away beyond the Mississippi River. Everyone was anxious to find new lands and a new life. The song *The Promised Land* was being sung by travelers on wagons, stagecoaches, flatboats, and later, on steamboats. It was sung around camp-fires and at camp meetings. The phrase, "I'm bound for the promised land," was on everyone's lips, and it was written in diaries and letters. Read the verses to the song. What do you think they tell about the land for which these travelers were searching?

The Promised Land

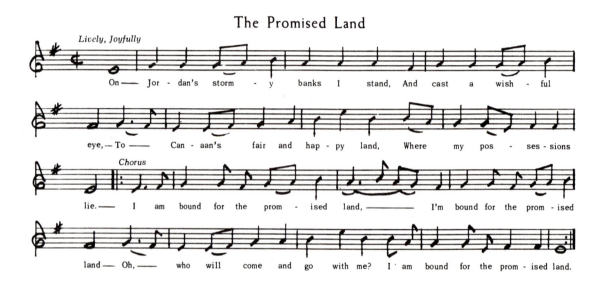

Lively, Joyfully

On — Jor - dan's storm - y banks I stand, And cast a wish - ful eye, — To — Can - aan's fair and hap - py land, Where my pos - ses - sions lie. — I am bound for the prom - ised land, — I'm bound for the prom - ised land — Oh, — who will come and go with me? I am bound for the prom - ised land.

2 There generous fruits that never fail
On trees immortal grow;
There rocks and hills and brooks and vales
With milk and honey flow.

Chorus: I am bound, etc.

3 O, the transporting rapt'rous scene
That rises to my sight
Sweet fields arrayed in living green
And rivers of delight.

Chorus: I am bound, etc.

Many pioneers traveled toward the promised land on keelboats. This drawing shows one way that these shallow, covered riverboats were made to move through the water. From the drawing you can see also how a keelboat was built. It could carry huge loads of freight, and it could be rowed, poled, or towed from the bank with a long rope pulled by horses, mules or men.

When the keelboat went downstream it drifted—though it was a chore to pole it safely through river rapids where the water dashed with white splashes against ledges and rocks. So ruggedly was a keelboat built, however, that it could take the shock of many collisions.

A sail on the stubby mast helped move the boat on windy days. But making the keelboat travel upriver was always difficult work. The crew, or the keelboatmen as they were called, had to place their long poles on the river bottom and push for all they were worth against the river current. This pushing moved the boat slowly, slowly up the river.

The steersman in the bow held a wide-bladed oar that served as a rudder. The broad, low cabin in the center of the boat was used as a resting place for crew or passengers, and for cargo. Sometimes the cabin was used as a shelter during an Indian attack! At such a time, crew and passengers poked rifles between the logs, took aim and fired.

The earliest keelboatmen were Frenchmen from fur-trading posts along the Mississippi River. However, it was not long before Americans learned to operate the keelboat. The boatmen were strong, loud, hardy men, rough in manner and appearance. They worked hard at a dangerous job in all kinds of weather. They commonly wore red shirts and were known as "red-shirted roarers." You can see that they were "first cousins" to the rowdy, stubble-faced wagoners on the National Pike.

As these river boatmen worked, they sang songs to make their work easier. Often they made up more verses to songs they already knew. Sometimes they created whole new songs!

This song, *Push Boat,* has a drowsy rhythm of poling. It tells about the thoughts that passed through the minds of the boatmen as they poled hour after hour. Read the words to the song. Try to imagine how the boatmen felt.

Push Boat

1. Go-ing up the riv-er From Cat-letts-burg to Pike, Work-ing on a push boat For old man Jeff-ry's Ike.

2. Working on a push boat
   For fifty cents a day,
   Buy my girl a brand new dress
   And throw the rest away.

3. Working on a push boat,
   Water's mighty slack,
   Taking sorghum 'lasses down,
   And bringing sugar back.

4. Pushing mighty hard, boys,
   Sand bar's in the way,
   Straining every muscle
   To get us off today.

5. I wish I had a nickel,
   I wish I had a dime,
   I'd spend it all on Cynthie Jane
   And dress her mighty fine.

6. The weather's mighty hot, boys,
   Blisters on my feet,
   Working on a push boat
   To buy my bread and meat.

7. Working on a push boat,
   Working in the rain,
   When I get to Catlettsburg,
   Good-by, Cynthie Jane.

A line, or company, of keelboats ran regular passenger and freight services on the Ohio River between Louisville, Cincinnati and Pittsburgh. They were called the Ohio River packets, because they carried packets of mail. One of their boats had a cannon on board for protection against Indian attacks.

Some folk tales and folk heroes grew out of the keelboat years. One of these heroes, Mike Fink, was called "King of the Keelboatmen." He became a living legend, like Daniel Boone and Davy Crockett. He boastfully described himself as "half horse, half alligator, and half snapping turtle." His colorful, adventurous deeds encouraged story tellers to weave them into "tall tales."

"Push Boat" from *Music in Our Country,* copyright 1956, 1962, Silver Burdett Company. Used by permission of the publisher and Jean Thomas, The Traipsin' Woman.

Here is one that tells about Mike Fink's skill in rifle shooting. Does it remind you of a similar story about a man and his son in another country?

The Shooting of the Cup

It all happened at one of those stopping points on the Ohio River, known by the name of "wooding places." The steamboat made a graceful turn towards the island above the wood chute and, rounding to, approached the woodpile, with the escape-steam sounding through the forest and hills like the bellowing of a caged tiger. The root of a tree prevented the boat from getting near the river bank, and it was necessary to use the paddles to take a different position.

"Back out, man, and try it again!" called a voice from the shore. "Throw your pole wide, and brace off, or you'll run against that snag!"

The speaker was immediately cheered by a dozen voices from the deck. He was leaning carelessly against a tree, his left arm pressing a rifle to his side. As he stood there, six feet tall and perfectly built, he resembled Hercules of old. Long exposure to the sun and weather on the lower Ohio and Mississippi Rivers had changed the color of his skin until he could have passed for the mightiest warrior of some powerful Indian tribe. Although at least fifty years of age, his hair was black as the wing of a crow. He wore a red flannel shirt, covered by a blue capot or coat trimmed with white fringe. On his feet were moccasins. Around his waist was

"The Shooting of the Cup" adapted from *A Treasury of American Folklore*, edited by B. A. Botkin. New York: Crown Publishers, Inc.

a broad leather belt from which hung a large knife in a sheath.

As soon as the steamboat was tied-up, the cabin passengers and crewmen jumped on shore.

The crewmen surrounded the big rifleman. "How are you, Mike?" they wanted to know.

Mike Fink replied by shaking their hands with squeezes like that of a blacksmith vise.

"I am glad to see you," he said in his abrupt way of speaking. "I was just going to shoot at the tin cup — and I want you to be the judges."

On any other occasion the steamboat

people from Philadelphia and Baltimore. The men decided to give them the opportunity of seeing a Western Lion — for such Mike Fink truly was — in all his glory.

Mike, followed by several of the keelboat crew, led the way to a grove of beech trees some distance from the boat landing. All passengers and crew members from the steamboat were invited to follow. On arriving at the spot, a stout boatmen who was the younger brother of Mike Fink drew a line in the dirt with his bare toe. From the line he stepped off thirty yards, then turned around to face Brother Mike. He took a tin cup, which hung from his belt, and placed it on his head.

men would have tried to prevent the daring trial of skill they knew was coming. But on their boat were two English tourists who were traveling over the United States to write a book about the customs and manners of Americans. Also on board were a few high-society

Then he said, "Blaze away, Mike! And let's win that bet!"

The passengers, as soon as they recovered from their astonishment, wanted to interfere. But Mike, throwing back his left leg for balance, leveled his rifle at the head of his brother. In this position, the rifle remained motionless for several seconds.

"Lower your piece a little or you'll lose that bet!" shouted his fearless brother.

In an instant, the sharp crack of a rifle was heard and the tin cup flew off thirty or forty yards — no longer fit for any use. The strangers rushed forward to see if the brother was really safe. He remained as immovable as if he had been made from stone. He had not even winked when the rifle ball struck the cup within two inches of his skull.

"Mike has won!" the strangers shouted.

No more excitement was exhibited among the keelboatmen than if a common, everyday bet had been won. In a few minutes, their "Keel" was seen wheeling into the current of the river — the giant form of Mike astride the large steering oar. As they left the shore, they gave an Indian yell and broke out into a sort of chorus beginning with —

"Hard upon the beech oar!

She moves too slow!

All the way to Shawneetown,

Long while ago."

See if you can find other stories about Mike Fink's daring adventures. This sharpshooting frontiersman led many lives. You may read about him not only as a keelboatman, but as an Indian scout, trapper and ranger. Some call him a hero of three frontiers because he moved from one frontier to another. Many stories have been written about his death. Perhaps you can find some of them to read. Which do you believe?

Downriver with Flatboats

After the War of 1812, jobs were scarce. The population was increasing, and restless citizens, bachelors and poor families packed their belongings and headed west, looking for a fresh start. Travel on the turnpikes was rigorous for town and city people, so they crowded the northern river ports, anxious to load their belongings on a keelboat or flatboat for the journey downriver. Some were seeking cheap land that was not too close to hostile Indians. Others were seeking fortune and adventure in whatever way and place they might find it.

One man, arriving in the present state of Illinois in 1818, described the country in a letter to his brother as a place where a man could enjoy himself, and where prairie land sixty miles long and ten broad could be bought for two dollars an acre. He once measured Indian corn more than fifteen feet high. He claimed he saw more peaches and apples rotting on the ground than would be needed to sink the British fleet. The flocks of turkeys, geese, ducks and hens would surprise anyone. And here, even the poorest family had a cow or two and some sheep.

El-a-noy

Way down u-pon the Wa-bash, Sich land was nev-er known, If A-dam had passed ov-er it, The soil he'd sure-ly own. He'd think it was the gar-den, He'd played in when a boy, And straight pro-nounce it E-den, In the State of El-a-noy.

Chorus

Then move your fam-ily west-ward, Good health you will en-joy, And rise to wealth and hon-or, In the State of El-a-noy.

She's bounded by the Wabash,
The Ohio and the Lakes,
She's crawfish in the swampy lands,
The milk-sick and the shakes;

But these are slight diversions,
And take not from the joy
Of living in this garden land,
The State of Elanoy.

CHORUS: Then move, *etc.*

Soon pioneers moving westward were singing the praises of Illinois in the song, *El-a-noy*. The words, "Then move your family westward, good health you will enjoy, and rise to wealth and honor . . . in the State of El-a-noy," probably influenced other families to go along.

It was expensive to rent the services of a keelboat and crew, so most families built or bought a flatboat to continue their journey. Many families sold most of their possessions and often borrowed more money to buy equipment and a flatboat. Booklets were sold in Pittsburgh that gave navigating instructions and information about bends in the river. Some pioneers had never traveled by river or navigated a flatboat piled high with belongings. Unfortunately, these river maps couldn't mark the shifting sand bars, or the "snags," which are logs or whole trees hung-up at places in the river. As a result, there were many tragedies among the travelers.

Nevertheless, the flatboat became the standard vehicle for traveling families. It was not as fast as a keelboat and was only a downstream boat, of course, and it could drift only with the current.

Besides the natural power of the river current, muscle-power of the settlers was often needed to move these rafts. Large-blade oars, called "sweeps" and push-poles helped keep the boat going. If a careful eye was not kept on the water ahead, the boat might run aground. Swirling rapids, hidden rocks, and snags could cause accidents or heavy damage.

But the flatboat, an Ohio River creation, was the frontier's most convenient and cheapest form of transportation. Sometimes at the end of a journey, the flatboat was broken up for lumber to build the settler's first frontier home.

The boat was the pioneers' chief defense against Indian attacks or river pirates. It had to be stoutly built and equipped with plenty of ammunition for the westward traveler to protect his family. Wise pioneers traveled in groups because of the danger of snags or Indian attacks.

Some called the raftlike flatboat an "ark." In many ways it did resemble Noah's Ark. But it allowed the pioneer's family to continue a normal life during the journey. Let's take a closer look at a rectangular, average-sized flatboat holding one family.

Livestock were penned up in one corner of the deck. These might include a horse, cattle, cows, hogs and chickens, all eating contentedly. The pioneer father and his young sons worked hard while handling the sweeps or push-poles. The enclosed large cabin, about four feet high, held all their supplies and worldly possessions. Sometimes a plow and farm tools were lashed to the cabin roof.

The family lived in the cabin. Even the cooking was done there over an open fire which could create a hazard, but which was necessary. The door and small windows allowed the smoke to escape. The windows, too, were used as portholes to fire at river pirates or attacking Indians.

Sometimes a wigwam instead of a cabin was seen on a flatboat deck. Regardless of the type of shelter, a heavy flatboat floating downriver was really a home on water. Children sometimes played on the cabin roof among a full line of drying clothes. The pioneer wife churned her butter just as she did while living on shore. When Indian attacks were less of a danger, some flatboats were merely a raft with fences on all sides and a shack in the middle.

People were usually happy as they drifted along because they were headed for a new home. They often sang, especially when they didn't have to worry about Indians.

The song *Noah's Ark* was sung by folks who were serious about their journey and others who joked about flatboats resembling arks.

Noah's Ark

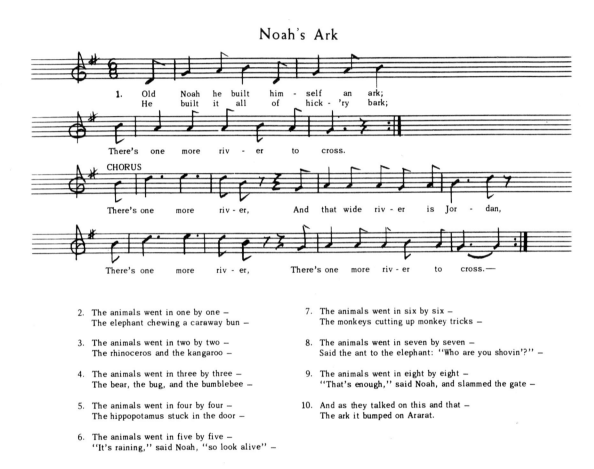

1. Old Noah he built him - self an ark;
   He built it all of hick - 'ry bark;
   There's one more riv - er to cross.

CHORUS

There's one more riv - er, And that wide riv - er is Jor - dan,
There's one more riv - er, There's one more riv - er to cross.—

2. The animals went in one by one —
   The elephant chewing a caraway bun —

3. The animals went in two by two —
   The rhinoceros and the kangaroo —

4. The animals went in three by three —
   The bear, the bug, and the bumblebee —

5. The animals went in four by four —
   The hippopotamus stuck in the door —

6. The animals went in five by five —
   "It's raining," said Noah, "so look alive" —

7. The animals went in six by six —
   The monkeys cutting up monkey tricks —

8. The animals went in seven by seven —
   Said the ant to the elephant: "Who are you shovin'?" —

9. The animals went in eight by eight —
   "That's enough," said Noah, and slammed the gate —

10. And as they talked on this and that —
    The ark it bumped on Ararat.

"Noah's Ark" from *Music Everywhere,* copyright 1944 by Summy-Birchard Company, Evanston, Illinois. Used by permission.

As a young man, Abraham Lincoln helped to build a flatboat, and contracted to take a load of hogs from New Salem, Illinois, to New Orleans. At that time the hogs of the region ran wild. Some were savage and very difficult to manage. When all the hogs had finally been gathered and penned, they wouldn't move an inch toward the boat.

Lincoln and his companions tried every method to get them on board, but nothing worked. One alternative was left. Lincoln actually carried them on board, one by one. His long arms and great strength helped him to transfer them rapidly, and off they went headed for New Orleans.

The streams of people who poured over the mountains into Ohio, Kentucky, Indiana, Illinois and Missouri founded numerous small communities. Many travelers continued on southern trails into Alabama, Mississippi and Arkansas.

Most professional boatmen sold their cargo and boat when they reached New Orleans. They walked home on the Natchez Trace or paddled upstream in dugout canoes.

This painting, sometimes called *The Jolly Boatmen,* shows some boatmen having a few moments of fun.

The Jolly Boatmen   *Library of Congress*

Most towns were located on rivers, but some were in farming centers. Soon business, manufacturing, and trade were flourishing. Again, flatboats were used to float salable goods to cities downriver. Can you find the names of some of these first American cities along the Ohio and Mississippi Rivers?

Many of the foreign immigrants from Scotland, Ireland, Germany, Switzerland, France and England came directly to the frontier with no backwoods experience. Their strange speech, folk customs, dress and ideas soon disappeared with the hard work of frontier life. Marriages between frontier young people of all nationalities, together with the warm, friendly welcome of the American settlers, helped these new Americans to find a better life in a new land.

Some of these new settlers from across the Atlantic Ocean brought folk songs with them that soon became known as American folk songs. One such song was *Barbara Allen*. Read it through before you sing it. What does it tell?

Barbara Allen

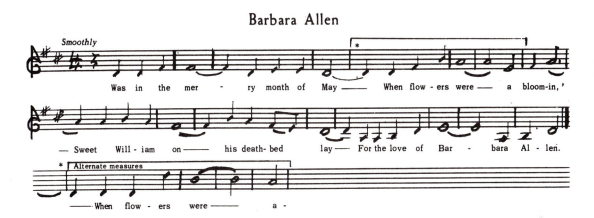

Was in the mer - ry month of May —— When flow-ers were —— a bloom-in,'
— Sweet Will - iam on —— his death-bed lay —— For the love of Bar - bara Al - len.

*Alternate measures
——·When flow-ers were —— a -

2. Slowly, slowly she got up,
   And slowly she went nigh him,
   And all she said when she got there,
   'Young man, I think you're dying.'

"Barbara Allen" from *The Folk Songs of North America* by Alan Lomax. Used by permission of The Richmond Organization, New York.

Low Bridge, Everybody Down

As a young man, George Washington tried to encourage settlers to move to the rich lands to the west. There were no railroads, of course, and roads were few and poor. Washington thought that short canals linking navigable rivers would ease a traveler's journey, and move the country's goods.

As a young surveyor, Washington supervised the building of a short canal used to move lumber through the Great Dismal Swamp of Virginia. You can see a drawing below of the way an artist pictured a hotel beside the canal. The artist used his imagination. Can you discover some things wrong with the picture? Do you think the sailboats and the steamboat would travel on a canal?

The Great Dismal Swamp Canal

Other great Americans, too, thought of digging canals to speed the westward trek. In 1772, Benjamin Franklin wrote in a letter, "Rivers are ungovernable things, especially in hilly countries. Canals are quiet and always manageable."

Early in our nation's history, short canals were dug and put to good use. Still, they were not of much use to the traveler who was going far west. A "far piece" of wagon travel had to be endured before he could reach the rivers and lakes which hastened his journey. People kept saying, "If only there was a long river flowing east to west!"

For eager Americans, then as now, to wish for a thing was the first step toward getting it. Since nature had provided no east-to-west waterway, they would make one.

And make one they did!

The Erie Canal, opened on October 26, 1825, ran west from Albany on the Hudson River to Buffalo on Lake Erie. It provided an almost level water route from the Atlantic Ocean across the Appalachian Mountain barrier to the Great Lakes.

The success of the Erie Canal made everyone canal-crazy. A network of inland waterways was built in New York, Connecticut, Delaware, Pennsylvania and Virginia. Often they paralleled the courses of unnavigable streams. By means of a series of canals, the Ohio River was connected to the Atlantic Ocean. Pioneers could reach the Ohio River easier and were that much closer to the western frontier.

Farmers from New York to Illinois enjoyed watching their cargo of produce being pulled along in a canal boat by a team of horses plodding the canal towpath. Canal transportation was used by passengers, too.

Since the canal was a public road, canal packets, or passenger boats, were owned by businessmen. To make their packets more appealing to the public, and to make their business venture more profitable, the boats were painted in bright colors. Shutters on the windows were painted in contrasting colors. The boats had a festive look.

Three groups of people traveled on a canal boat. First, there were those who

Traveling by Canal Boat

were really going some place, such as the pioneers heading West. They slept below and, when possible, brought their own food; otherwise, the canal boat owner's wife would cook their meals in her tiny kitchen. The second group came aboard gaily just to travel to the next town. They thought of a canal boat as an outing craft to ride for pleasure. Laughing ladies held parasols over their heads to keep from getting too much sun. They enjoyed the slow trip, admiring the beautiful scenery just as we enjoy a walk through the countryside today. The third group was made up of businessmen and families who wanted to travel to a nearby city on the canal route.

Travel on the "Big Ditch," as the Erie Canal was sometimes called, provided more comforts than a stagecoach or other means of overland travel. Packets moved about four miles an hour and charged fares of from three cents to four cents a mile. For this, passengers received their meals and a bed in which to sleep. The meals were so good that captains had to watch for "spongers" who would sneak on board for a "free" meal and then quietly slip away. One passenger who traveled from Schenectady to Buffalo wrote that his dinner included four or five kinds of meat and fowl, a variety of hot breads, enormous bowls of vegetables, and seven or eight kinds of cake or pie. A closely-packed, jolting stagecoach wasn't as accommodating.

With the horses or mules pulling on the towpath, the ride on a canal boat was slow and peaceful. Excitement was in the form of passing another boat, reaching a town or going under a bridge. Before passing under a bridge, the helmsman would toot a horn and call out "bridge," "*very* low bridge," "low, low bridge," or "the *lowest* in the canal." At this time it was up to every passenger to bend low or to lie flat on deck. The words to the song *Erie Canal* describe such a scene.

The Erie Canal

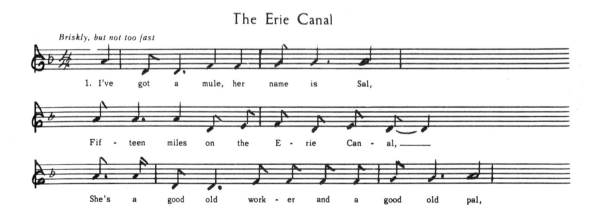

Fif - teen miles on the E - rie Can - al.

We've hauled some barg — es in our day,

Filled with lum — ber, coal and hay, And

we know ev - 'ry inch of the way From

Al - ba - ny to Buf — fa - lo.

Refrain

Low bridge, ev - 'ry - bod - y down!

Low bridge, for we're go - ing thro' a town.

And you'll al - ways know your neigh - bor,

You'll al - ways know your pal,

If you ev - er nav - i - gat - ed on the E - rie Can - al.

2. We better get along our way,
Fifteen miles on the Erie Canal,
'Cause you bet your life I'd never part with Sal,
Fifteen miles on the Erie Canal.
Git up there, mule, — here comes a lock,
We'll make Rome 'bout six o'clock —
One more trip and back we'll go —
Right back home to Buffalo.

Gradually, many towns began to spring up along the canals. Travelers on their way West, finding a place that they liked before they arrived at their planned destination, would decide to stay there. The population grew along the canals for another reason. People knew that by living close to it they could send their produce to market, as well as receive supplies from the East. They felt they could keep in touch with bigger cities and civilization because they were near this form of transportation.

The "Ohio Fever" had gripped many settlers who lived near the canal. The slow movement through the locks discouraged no one. People still headed West. It was only during the winter months, when the canals were locked in ice, that overland routes were used for trade and transport.

Some pioneers traveled the Erie Canal down the Hudson River to New York City. From here they could go around the world or to California by clipper ship.

The *Clermont*

Steamboat: Wedding Cake on Water

In 1807, Robert Fulton's *Clermont* was the first successful steamboat in the United States. Doubtful spectators who gathered to watch its trial run were amazed when it furiously began to churn water and slowly chugged upstream *against the current and without wind power or manpower!* The *Clermont*, or "Fulton's Folly," soon completely changed traffic on rivers, lakes, and oceans the world around.

Here is an artist's drawing of the *Clermont* landing at the village of Cornwall on the Hudson River about 1810. Compare it with the "floating palaces" found on the Mississippi River.

The steamboat was described as an engine on a raft with about $10,000 worth of wood, tin, shingles, canvas and twine around it. Some said that if a steamboat should go to sea, the ocean would take one swift slap at it and people would be picking up its pieces on shore for years to come.

But at first the steamboats did not go to sea. They moved on the river where the water was calmer. For some years they carried most of the freight and passengers for the great Middle West. However, when the railroad came along the steamboats were put out of business. Only a few can be seen in the United States today. Most of them run on the rivers for pleasure and for tourist excursions.

Why do you suppose a steamboat is called "she"? Many reasons have been given by Mississippi River old-timers. Some say it is because it takes a smart man to manage her. Others say, with a chuckle, that no two of them act alike and need a little touching up with paint now and then to look just right. Another reason, in a more serious vein, claims it is because a steamboat moves with such dignity and grace. This may be true, for no other kind of transportation has had such romance and glamour attached to it.

Mississippi River Steamboats   *Los Angeles County Museum*

Some people have described the large, sidewheel steamboat as looking like a beautiful swan sitting gracefully upon the water. Two such steamboats, the *Diana* and *Baltic,* are shown in this picture. They seem to be moving along a narrow river channel. Could they be engaged in a race?

Imagine these steamboats painted a glistening white with a trim of blue or red. The main cabin, which extended nearly the full length of the boat, was decorated in white and gold. Travelers enjoyed strolling about a steamboat to admire the furnishings which included French mirrors in hand-carved gold frames, Persian rugs, marble-topped tables, velvet upholstered chairs and settees, a fine piano, orchestras, murals and a real barber shop. In a steamboat dining room, the crystal chandeliers had oil lamps set in them. No wonder such boats were called floating palaces.

A Steamboat Dining Room

With the coming of the steamboat, the need for keelboats and flatboats did not end immediately because passengers and cargoes continued to drift downriver. But now people needing to return upriver could "steam" back.

The great popularity of the steamboat, from about 1820 to 1870, has caused these years to be referred to as the "Steamboat Era." Certain river towns grew with the hustle and bustle of the steamboat business. Cities such as Cincinnati, Pittsburgh, St. Louis, New Orleans, Natchez and Memphis became the starting point or the landing place for many Western-bound travelers.

Pittsburgh, a great inland port, was once called the Gateway to the West. As the frontier moved westward, the title shifted to St. Louis. But in 1840 a steady stream of people crowded the Pittsburgh waterfront waiting to board a steamboat. Their journey began down the Ohio River. At the Mississippi River junction some would continue northwest on the Missouri River, and some would go south on the Mississippi. Some people first traveled by canalboat and flatboat and then transferred to a steamboat, especially if the steamboat was headed upriver.

The flatboatmen in this picture are resting as steamboats pass. The steamboat in the foreground is a stern-wheeler, while the one in the distance is a side-wheeler. Can you explain this difference?

Watching the Steamboats Pass

Steamboats were always in danger of getting caught on one of the shifting sand bars. When going through shallow water it was necessary to measure the depth at regular intervals. This was called "taking soundings." When soundings had to be taken, a long rope weighted with a pipe filled with lead was dropped into the river from the boat's prow. The "lead line" was marked at intervals to measure depth. The sounding man, or leadman, recognized these marks as the rope slid through his hands in the darkness. He called out the soundings in a sing-song chant as the line dropped.

"Quarter less four" means 22½ feet; "half twain" is 15 feet; "quarter twain" means 13½ feet; "mark twain" is 12 feet (two fathoms, safe water); "quarter less twain" means 10½ feet. Measurements less than "quarter less twain" are given in number of feet. The job of the "sounding man" stationed on the prows of Mississippi paddle-wheelers was to keep the boat from getting stuck on a sandbar. One "sounding man" later became a famous American author. He used as his pen name the sounding call, "Mark Twain," which meant two fathoms. What do you know about this man?

Mississippi Sounding Calls

Quar-ter less four, —— Half twain, —— Quar-ter twain, —— Mark twain, ——

Quar-ter less twain, —— Nine and a half feet, —— Nine feet, ——

Eight and a half feet. ——

"Mississippi Sounding Calls" from *Archive of Folk Song*, Record 8LP recorded by Herbert Halpert, Library of Congress, Washington, D. C. Reprinted from *A Treasury of Mississippi River Folklore*, edited by B. A. Botkin, Crown Publishers, Inc., 1955.

Many steamboats moved on the Hudson River between Albany and New York. The folk song, *Hudson River Steamboat*, might have been sung by Hudson River travelers.

Hudson River Steamboat

2. Shadboat, pickle boat Lying side by side,
   Fisher folk and sailormen, Waiting for the tide,
   Rain cloud, storm cloud, Over yonder hill.
   Thunder on the Dunderberg, Rumbles in the *Kill.*

3. The "Sedgewick" was racing And she lost all hope,
   Used up her steam On the big calliope,
   But she hopped right along, She was hopping quick.
   All the way from Stony Point to Pappaloppen Creek.

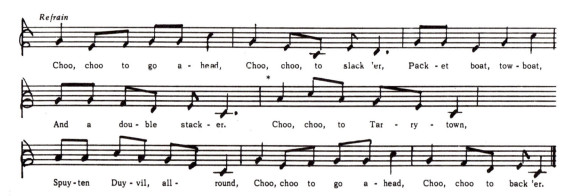

REFRAIN　2. Choo, choo to go ahead, Choo, choo, to slack 'er,
            Packet boat, towboat, And a double stacker.
        * Choo, choo, to Tarrytown, Spuyten Duyvil, all round,
            Choo, choo to go ahead, Choo, choo to back 'er.

          3. Choo, choo to go ahead, Choo, choo, to slack 'er,
            Packet boat, towboat, And a double stacker.
        * New York to Albany, Round out and Tivoli,
            Choo, choo to go ahead, Choo, choo to back 'er.

Not only were westward travelers grateful for the steamboat, but farmers, settlers, and businessmen now had reasonable transportation. They were able to get Eastern products in quantity, and they could ship their own products to market inexpensively.

Southern plantation owners filled the holds of steamboats with their cotton and sugar to be shipped to northern river ports. Fortunes were made by plantation owners and by owners of steamboats. Steamboat travel, however, was dangerous. Steamboats caught on fire. Their boilers exploded. They sank when they ran against rocks and snags, or broke up when they ran aground on sand bars. A steamboat lasted from two to ten years. On the "crazy" Missouri River, the *average* was only four years. But if a steamboat remained in service for three years the owner usually showed a profit.

It was a sad day for passengers to view the hulk of a favorite boat rotting in the river. These rotting hulks apparently bothered a timid old lady on board a steamboat. As the story goes, she approached the captain and said anxiously, "Is it true that a great many men have been drowned in this river?"

The captain calmed her when he replied, "Dear madam, do not believe everything you hear. I assure you I have never met a man who has been drowned in the Mississippi River."

The social life aboard a steamboat attracted many travelers. There was something on board for everyone's taste. A gambler could spend his days and nights at the gaming tables. Some folk strolled the decks and admired the scenery, danced in the ballrooms, or listened contentedly to the music of the orchestras.

Many travelers spent most of their time in the dining room, eating. The food on a steamboat seemed to be unusually fine. Famous chefs were valued and steamboat owners competed for their services. Menus had an international flavor: seven soups, scores of main dishes, and fifteen different desserts. All of this luxury in a country where bear meat, coon and possum had so recently been the daily fare!

This story is told by many river travelers. You might enjoy reading it, too.

The crew and officers of one of the finest river steamers had been noticing something they found impossible to explain. One passenger, an elderly, jovial man, had taken one of the best cabins and had remained on board for several round-trips between St. Louis and New Orleans. They knew he wasn't a gambler, adventurer or fugitive. He seemed to be a fine, pleasant person who had formed many friendships on board. Finally the captain asked him why he had remained on board so long.

The man's answer became historic. "Why, Captain, it's the finest way to enjoy myself that I know. No American hotel can equal this—your menu of the finest food —wild game, your glazed fish, your roasts, sauces and desserts! My finely decorated cabin, the bar and promenade—nothing matches them. And the friends I meet, the best people in the world. Why should I leave?"

The enormous steamboats of the Ohio and Mississippi required a great deal of fuel. Wood was cut and piled on shore by woodcutters hired by the steamboat line. When the boat stopped at a huge pile to "wood up," the woodcutters carried many loads of wood on board. This stop gave passengers the opportunity to go on shore for a stroll. But snakes under the woodpile frightened many of the passengers, and they hastily returned on board.

Woodcutters lived on shore all along the thousand mile river bank. Sometimes friendly Indians offered to cut wood, too, for a fee.

The virgin forests provided years of fuel, but later, when the wood supply was gone, the mines in Pennsylvania provided coal for the steamboats. The woodcutters then became shantyboat men or moved to farms.

The steamboat changed westward travel habits. It speeded up the journey over long stretches. Travel became an exciting vacation for many people. It helped to develop different kinds of businesses on the frontier by transporting both people and supplies.

The river song, *Down the Ohio*, could have been sung by river travelers on flat-boats and steamboats. The happy rhythm shows how eager pioneers were to get "down the Ohio" and farther toward the West.

Down the Ohio

Joyously DESCANT

Swish   swish   swish   swish,

MELODY

The riv-er is up and the chan-nel is deep, The wind is stead-y and strong,

Swish   swish   swish   swish. Oh,

Oh, won't we have a jol-ly good time As we — go sail-ing a-long.

Refrain

Down the riv-er, Oh, down the riv-er, Oh, down the riv-er we go-o-o.

Down the riv-er, Oh, down the riv-er, Oh, down the O-hi-o! —

"Down the Ohio" used by permission of Lynn Rohrbough, Cooperative Recreation Service, Inc., Delaware, Ohio.

Sailing Ship Days

The Yankee skipper on a sailing vessel was a man who believed in strict discipline. The sailor's work was hard and never-ending: washing down decks, manning the pumps, pounding oakum, climbing a rigging in an icy gale to take in the sails.

Chantey-singing helped the seamen at their work. The clearly measured rhythm set the timing for such tasks as weighing anchor and hoisting sail. These were tasks that required exact teamwork.

The chanteyman was a member of the crew whose voice and memory singled him out above all others. Most of the songs had solo parts that were sung by the chanteyman while the sailors were getting their grip on the line. Then, on the chorus, all hands pulled together. Without the rhythm of the music, the heave or drag would not have had the exact timing needed to throw the entire weight of every man on the line at the same instant.

The chanteys were of several varieties. The "short-drag" chanteys, like *Haul On The Bowline*, were sung when only a few rapid, heavy pulls were required. "Windlass" chanteys were those used for a long, steady process like hoisting anchor. "Halyard" chanteys, like *Blow, Boys, Blow*, were used for longer, heavier tasks such as hoisting sail.

As you read the words to this halyard chantey, try to picture the chanteyman and the sailors at their task. Then sing the song as you think it was sung aboard an early sailing vessel or ship.

Blow the Man Down

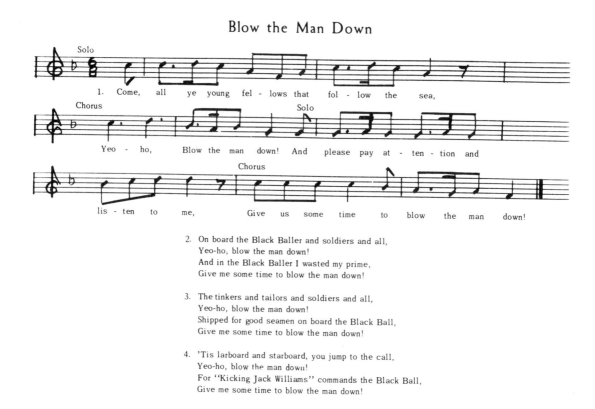

1. Come, all ye young fel-lows that fol-low the sea, Yeo-ho, Blow the man down! And please pay at-ten-tion and lis-ten to me, Give us some time to blow the man down!

2. On board the Black Baller and soldiers and all,
   Yeo-ho, blow the man down!
   And in the Black Baller I wasted my prime,
   Give me some time to blow the man down!

3. The tinkers and tailors and soldiers and all,
   Yeo-ho, blow the man down!
   Shipped for good seamen on board the Black Ball,
   Give me some time to blow the man down!

4. 'Tis larboard and starboard, you jump to the call,
   Yeo-ho, blow the man down!
   For "Kicking Jack Williams" commands the Black Ball,
   Give me some time to blow the man down!

In addition to chanteys, which were actual work songs, sailors sang for enjoyment when they were off-duty. The songs that were sung for pure pleasure were called "forecastle songs" because the sailors gathered on the fore, or front part, of the deck to sing them. One of their favorite songs was *Blow, Ye Winds*.

Blow, Ye Winds

1. 'Tis ad-ver-tised in Bos-ton, New York and Buf-fa-lo,

Five hun-dred brave A-mer-i-cans, A-whal-ing for to go, sing-ing:

Refrain

Blow, ye **winds, in the** morn-ing, Blow, ye winds, heigh-ho,

Haul a-way your run-ing gear, And blow, ye winds, heigh-ho.

2. They send you to New Bedford, That famous whaling port,
   And give you to some land sharks To board and fit you out, singing:
   Refrain

3. And now we're out to sea, my boys, The wind comes on to blow;
   One half the watch is sick on deck, The other half below, singing:
   Refrain

4. The skipper's on the quarter-deck, Squintin' at the sails,
   When, up above, the lookout sights A mighty school of whales, singing:
   Refrain

5. And now that he is ours, my boys, We'll tow him alongside;
   Then over him with our blubber-hooks, And rob him of his hide, singing:
   Refrain

A Clipper Ship

Westward by Clipper Ships

The slow and difficult method of moving westward in wagons, on horseback or on foot did not appeal to people who wanted an easier and faster way to travel. Many of these people booked passage on sailing vessels called clipper ships. Migration to the West was greatly helped by ocean winds as they filled the great sails of these ships that were loaded with passengers and cargo bound for California. However, during storms at sea, there were many times when these same winds were troublemakers.

Sometimes only the will of the skipper and the skill of the sailors kept a ship afloat. And sometimes even this wasn't enough. Many ships were lost in the long, dangerous voyage around Cape Horn at the foot of South America and up the Pacific coast to California. Many ships that sailed were dirty, rat-infested, and not seaworthy. However, men were willing to take the chance of sailing on them, particularly after 1848, because they were impatient to reach California and its rich gold fields. Despite the many hardships of traveling on such ships, men would joke about taking along their own grave stones. They helped to pass the time aboard by singing songs like this one.

Sailing for San Francisco

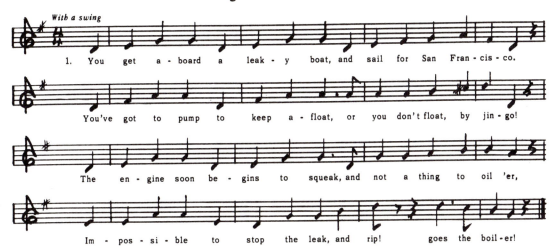

With a swing

1. You get a-board a leak-y boat, and sail for San Fran-cis-co.

You've got to pump to keep a-float, or you don't float, by jin-go!

The en-gine soon be-gins to squeak, and not a thing to oil 'er,

Im-pos-si-ble to stop the leak, and rip! goes the boil-er!

2. Oh, pork and beans they can't afford to second cabin passengers;
   The cook has fallen overboard with forty pounds of sassengers;
   The engineer is not too bright, he's bragging on the mail-line;
   He fin'lly gets into a fight, and rip! goes the enjine!

"Sailing for San Francisco" from *This Is Music*, Book 5, by William R. Sur, Robert E. Nye, William R. Fisher, and Mary R. Tolbert. Copyright 1962, 1967, Allyn and Bacon, Inc. Used by permission.

The long, slender clipper ships were truly things of beauty as they "clipped" through the water under full sail.

Museum of Early American Folk Art

This fine portrait of a clipper ship captain was painted about 1835. He is holding a collapsible telescope. It was an important tool for his particular kind of work. Why was the telescope such a useful instrument to the captain of a clipper ship?

A folk tale that might have been told by passengers and sailors during the long journey on a clipper ship is about the Gloucester sea serpent. Many tales of this kind were told about strange creatures in the sea. Can you explain how such stories might have originated?

The Gloucester Sea Serpent

It was in the summer of 1817 that, for a period of two weeks, an enormous sea serpent was seen in the harbor of Gloucester, Massachusetts, as well as in near-by monster-haunted Nahant Bay. So many people saw it and agreed in describing how it looked that a thrill of fear swept the coast of New England,

and a reward was posted for its capture, dead or alive.

The monster reptile was usually seen lolling in the waves, with the arches of its back sticking out of the water. Sometimes it moved rapidly, and sometimes it only lazed along, but in any case it was a frightening sight. It seemed to be about 100 feet long and three feet or a little less around, although one skipper said positively that the monster was as long as the mainmast of a 74-gun ship of the line. Another skipper claimed that it took him fifteen minutes to sail the length of the reptile, even with a six-knot breeze blowing and all sail on.

The serpent often was seen by a number of people at the same time. Sometimes it was a mile away; at other times, only a few yards. Everyone agreed that it had a smooth black or dark brown skin, and several said that they had seen a long tongue sticking out from its snake-like head. The eye, one person said, was like that of an ox. Usually the serpent was seen in the water, but a couple of times it was seen, or thought to be seen, half in the water and half on shore.

As news of the monster spread, people by the hundreds rushed to the beaches whenever its presence was reported. Some were brave enough to go out in small boats to try for a closer look. Whalers in larger craft were trying to get the reward for its capture. Nets were spread. The men on board a government cutter were ordered to watch for the beast with guns at the ready. The serpent was fired at, according to one witness who claimed he got close enough to empty his duck gun at its head.

The monster seemed unaware of anything around it or of the people, regardless of whether they were trying to harm it or were just curious. Nor did it ever make any sound. Later it was seen moving south toward Nahant and it reappeared in Long Island Sound. Then it dropped from sight and history.

Can you find other stories about sea monsters? If so, read them.

An Ocean Going Steamship *Los Angeles County Museum*

Clipper ships were fast sailing vessels. With their "mile-high" masts and "acres" of canvas sail, they could make the long voyage to California in one-half the time required by older-style ships. One hundred days from Boston to San Francisco was a good run. The Yankee Clippers were in general use until the 1850's when ocean going steamships began to take over most of the ocean travel and trade.

When gold was discovered in California, ships were hard-pressed to serve the west coast. A plan was developed for transporting passengers by ship to the Isthmus of Panama. There they were unloaded on the Atlantic side and taken fifty miles across the neck of land where ships, waiting on the Pacific side, carried them on to California.

The search for gold didn't always help ocean transportation. It was not unusual for a ship's crew, and sometimes even the captain, to abandon their ship when they reached California. They hurried to buy a pick and a certain kind of pan for washing gold. Then they made their way to the hills and streams in search of the thing that they thought was going to make them rich. Men on their way to the gold fields were excited and happy. Often they sang as they hurried along. What do the words of this song tell you about their hopes and dreams?

The Forty-Niners

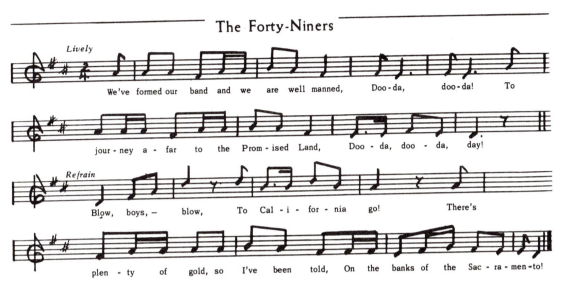

We've formed our band and we are well manned, Doo-da, doo-da! To jour-ney a-far to the Prom-ised Land, Doo-da, doo-da, day!

Refrain

Blow, boys, — blow, To Cal-i-for-nia go! There's plen-ty of gold, so I've been told, On the banks of the Sac-ra-men-to!

2. Where the golden ore is rich in store, Dooda, dooda!
On the banks of the Sacramento shore, Dooda, dooda, day!

3. As the gold is thar most any whar, Dooda, dooda!
And they dig it out with an iron bar, Dooda, dooda, day!

4. And whar 'tis thick, with a spade or pick, Dooda, dooda!
They can take out lumps as heavy as a brick, Dooda, dooda, day!

"The Forty-Niners," or "Sacramento," from *Music in Our Country,* copyright 1956, 1962, Silver Burdett Company. Used by permission.

Flatboat and Keelboat Travel Activities

1. Make a model of a flatboat. Demonstrate how the pioneers used poles to keep it moving downriver.

2. Pretend that you are a member of a large family and that you are helping to load the family possessions on a flatboat for the trip downriver to your new home. Write a story and draw pictures to describe your journey.

3. You are in charge of a keelboat crew and the boat is stuck on a snag or tree trunk in the river. Indians have been shooting at you from the banks. Then they suddenly surround you in their canoes. Write or tell how you save your crew and yourself.

4. On a map, trace the course of Abraham Lincoln's flatboat load of hogs from New Salem, Illinois, on the Sangamon River, to New Orleans.

5. Suppose that you have reached New Orleans safely with a flatboat load of hogs and farm produce. You have sold everything, even the logs of your raft, for a good price. Before you start back upriver, you decide to visit the city of New Orleans. Describe what you saw. (You will need to read about Old New Orleans and the kind of people who lived there.)

6. Read other tall tales about Mike Fink. Draw pictures to illustrate these tales.

7. Look in music books for other folk songs about flatboats and keelboats. Sing some of these songs for the class.

8. Suppose you are a boy or girl on a flatboat that drifts downriver day after day for several weeks. What would you do to amuse yourself?

9. Suppose you and your family were floating downriver and came upon two children clinging to a log in the water. You and your father manage to swing the raft around so you can rescue the two children. They tell you that their raft had broken to pieces when it hit a sand bar. They don't know what happened to the other members of the family. Write a story and explain what happened to the children.

Canal Boat Days Activities

1. Pretend that you are the Captain of an Erie Canal boat. Describe what you would do if a fire broke out inside the cabin.

2. Draw some humorous pictures of people trying to load their animals aboard canal barges.

3. Do a research project on the building of canals. Select one canal to describe to the class.

4. Find additional folk songs that were sung during the time that canal boat travel was popular.

5. Make a model of canal locks. Demonstrate how the locks work.

6. Pretend that you are a boy whose mule is supposed to pull a boat along the canal. The mule refuses to budge. Other boats are coming, and the people on board are shouting at you. Write a story telling what you would do.

7. Make up a poem or a song about traveling on a canal boat.

Steamboat Days Activities

1. Do a research project on Robert Fulton and describe his "Folly."

2. Build models of steamboats. Explain the difference between a stern-wheeler and a side-wheeler.

3. Read about steamboat races on the Mississippi. Describe these races to the class.

4. Look in music books and find other folk songs that were sung along the Mississippi River during steamboat days. Learn some of those songs in class.

5. Find information about the great cotton plantations along the rivers. Draw or collect pictures of plantation homes. Make a scrapbook to share with your classmates.

6. Select as a project, "Negro Folk Songs." Include examples of all types of songs: spirituals, work songs, play-party songs and jazz. Try to explain the meaning of each song in your report.

7. Pretend that you are a visitor to the United States from Europe and that you are traveling down the Mississippi River to New Orleans. Write a story about your experiences. Draw some cartoons to illustrate your story.

8. Find information about the "minstrel shows" and the showboats that traveled the Mississippi River. Help plan a minstrel show for your class to present.

9. Select "Louisiana Folklore" as a topic. Find songs, stories, games and dances that were enjoyed by the French people of Louisiana.

Clipper Ship and Ocean Steamboat Travel Activities

1. Make a model of an early sailing vessel. Give the history of the particular ship you have chosen.

2. Find additional tall tales of sailing ship days in books at the library. Recommend some for the class to read.

3. Collect or draw pictures of sailing ships for a scrapbook. Include interesting information about each kind of ship.

4. Pretend that you have made the dangerous trip around the Horn on a sailing ship. As soon as you reach San Francisco, write a letter to your parents in New York, telling them about your voyage.

5. You are an adventurous young writer who wants to live through some exciting experiences so you can write about them in a book. You go aboard a leaky, over-crowded, dirty old sailing vessel on May 15, 1850, to make the long voyage around South America. You have many carefree, gold-hungry companions. You make notes in your diary all during the long voyage until you reach San Francisco on October 10, 1850. Share your diary with the class. (Where will you find information that will help you with your notes?)

6. Look in music books for more sea-chanteys. Perhaps the class can learn to sing some of them.

7. On a large scale map, trace the course of a traveler who takes the Isthmus of Panama route from Boston to California. Remember, this was long before the Panama Canal was built and before there was a railroad. There were fever swamps and jungles to cross. Do you think you would make the crossing by river boat or by trail?

CHAPTER III

WAGON TRAILS WESTWARD

Life on the Texas Frontier

In 1821, an American, Stephen Austin, acquired a parcel of land as large as some of our small states. This land was near the place where the city of Houston, Texas, is located today. Stephen Austin agreed to bring in three hundred families, but he did better than that. In ten years, almost five thousand American settlers lived on his land.

Other Americans founded or started additional colonies. By 1836, Texas had almost 35,000 American settlers. A few came from as far away as New England, but most of the settlers were southerners interested in growing cotton. Many came to Texas reasonably prosperous, and brought Negro slaves with them. One such, William Wilson, brought his family from Charleston, South Carolina. Coming to the frontier from the kind of life enjoyed by the aristocrats of the South must have been very difficult. The first homes were cabins. Much of the household furniture had to be made by hand. Chairs had frames and rawhide seats. Other pieces of furniture were rough copies of those back home.

Perhaps you would like to read about some of the experiences of the Wilson family. Remember as you read this story that this was a reasonably wealthy family from Charleston, which was the center of social life for Southern aristocrats. William Wilson was an adventurous young father who wanted to move West to grow cotton. His wife was from the Calhoun family. Many of her people, including John C. Calhoun, were leaders among Southern statesmen. As a good wife, she knew that she had to go with her husband. She did not anticipate the many hardships that she would have to endure. After all, they took with them many Negroes to do the hard work. There were even Negro women to take care of her young children.

Arriving in Texas after an exhausting journey by boat and across swampy land, the Wilson family settled in Northeastern Texas far from any trade center. The walls of a rough cabin were quickly built. Before the roof was on, it was necessary for William Wilson and some of his men to go back to the river port to haul more of their possessions.

Mrs. Wilson, with her small children and the rest of their Negro slaves, were warned to stay inside the cabin at night since there were raiding parties of hostile Comanche Indians in the area.

That first night, after the dogs were put outside and the door bolted, everyone lay down in the roofless cabin and tried to sleep with the stars shining in their eyes. Sometime during the night the dogs began to whine under the cabin.

Indians? Or just some harmless animals new to the dogs? It was Indians, as they discovered when a war-painted Comanche climbed the wall and started to jump over. Mrs. Wilson shot her rifle —and missed.

What the rifle failed to accomplish, a Negro accomplished with an axe. As fast as an Indian showed above the wall, he was driven back with the axe. This was too much for the Indians. They ran away, contenting themselves with stealing the horses.

This young mother lived to tell about a very frightening experience. Her Negro slave had saved all their lives.

There were many happenings of this kind on the frontier, but like other American pioneers, the Wilson family possessed the courage and will to succeed.

They paid a high price. Two of the Wilson children contracted the dreaded fever. They were far from medical help and the children died. The mother was saddened, too, because her other children were growing up without formal schooling. They had to be taught at home because there were no schools. The same was true for religious training.

This proud and aristocratic mother found it difficult to accept the rough frontier manners of people who came to their home. She dreamed about sending their sons back home or to England to be educated. But the sons became true frontiersmen and loved to live on the huge cattle and cotton ranch.

Mrs. Wilson never quite reconciled herself to the rough Texas life, especially as her children began to find mates among the frontier people—people quite unprepared to become a part of the Wilson family, so she thought. However, her children and grandchildren found their place as the area continued to be settled. Most of them became cattle ranchers and several were among those who drove herds over the long trails to the "railheads" in Kansas.

Cattle Trails to the North

There were no cattle in America before the white man came. Spanish cattle were brought to the New World by Columbus and by other explorers. These long-horned cattle thrived on Mexican ranches. Herds were later driven into the grasslands of Texas. They were the ancestors of the famous Texas "longhorns."

When the railroad was built through to Abilene and Dodge City in Kansas, the Texas cattlemen began to drive their herds of longhorns to these frontier towns. From there, the cattle were shipped by train to meat-packing plants in Kansas City and Chicago.

The railroads gave cattlemen new shipping points. Sidney and Ogallala in Nebraska, Pine Bluffs and Cheyenne in Wyoming, and Glendive and Miles City in Montana all became "cow towns."

These towns were filled with "whoop-it-up" cowhands wanting to "soak up a little sociability," and looking for ways to spend their money after the long, hard cattle drives. "Tin-horn" gamblers, con-men, and drifters of all kinds were there to oblige them. Stockyard agents were there to buy cattle, along with wagon freighters, soldiers, Indians, and gun fighters drifting through. All in all, these roaring cow towns were centers of much trouble for frontier lawmen.

Tales of rustlers and cattle wars are a part of our American legends today. Except in songs like this one, "cowboys" seldom referred to themselves as such. Only in fun did they call each other "cowpuncher" or "cowpoke." It wasn't until after the railroad came that such names were heard, and then usually in joking. These workers preferred to be called "cowhands."

Black Tail Range

Medium swing

1. I am a rov-ing cow-boy From off the west-ern plains, My trade is cinch-ing sad-dles And pull-ing bri-dle reins. I can throw a las-so With grace-ful-ness and ease, And I can rope a bron-co And ride him where I please.

3. Won't ever go a-mining
   I'll stay here punching cows,
   And keep my hoss and saddle
   And watch the longhorns browse.
   Won't use a pick and shovel
   Won't start out with a whoop,
   Won't have to walk so far that
   My toe pokes through my boot.

4. I am a roving cowboy,
   I'm wearing buckskin chaps,
   I pack a big six-shooter,
   And I don't mean perhaps.
   I'm a roving cowboy,
   Won't ever, ever change,
   I'll stay right here prospecting
   On good old Black Tail Range.

The Night Herdsman

Ranching was a lonely business amid vast spaces. Cowhands sang to keep themselves and their cattle company, to entertain their friends, and to "let off steam." When a cattleman was asked why cowhands always sang to the cattle while riding around a herd at night, he explained that it was to let the cattle know that someone was around looking after their safety. On the range, everything was very quiet at night. Any sudden noise might awaken cattle and frighten them. Then they were apt to jump and run, causing a "stampede."

A night-man, riding around and around the cattle as they slept, whistled or sang in a low voice. If he happened to disturb the cattle in this quiet kind of way, they would hear him and go back to sleep after he passed. Cowhands enjoyed many kinds of songs. One that might have been sung to quiet cattle is the *Night Herding Song.* Read the words and listen to the melody. Do you think it would have a calming effect on the herd of cattle shown in the picture above?

Night-Herding Song

Slow, lilting

1. Oh, slow up dog-ies, quit rov-ing a-round, You have wand-ered and tram-pled all ov-er the ground; Oh graze a-long, dog-ies, and feel kind-a slow, And don't for-ev-er be on the go. Oh, move slow, dog-ies, move slow. Hi-oo, hi-oo,

1st and others Hi-oo!

last oo!

2. I've circle-herded and night-herded too,
   But to keep you together, that's what I can't do;
   My horse is leg-weary and I'm awful tired,
   But if you get away, I am sured to get fired,
   Bunch up, little dogies, bunch up,
   Hi-oo, hi-oo, hi-oo!

3. Oh, lie still dogies, since you have lain down,
   Stretch away out on the big open ground;
   Snore loud, little dogies, and drown the wild sound,
   That will all go away when the day rolls around.
   Lie still little dogies, lie still,
   Hi-oo, hi-oo, hi-oo!

Between 1870 and 1890 it is estimated that as many as twelve million head of cattle were driven up the Old Chisholm Trail from Texas and Arkansas. The weeks and months on horseback offered little to relieve the men from the heat, the rain and the monotony. Singing helped to pass the long, weary hours. The jogging, loping and cantering rhythms of the horses sometimes changed the pattern of an old song from some other place to a special kind of song to fit the cowhands' kind of work.

A sailor, who had decided to become a cowhand, sang his new friends an old ballad of the sea that began with the line, "Oh bury me not in the deep, deep sea." The cowhands liked the song and changed it to fit their life on "the lone prairie."

The Lone Prairie

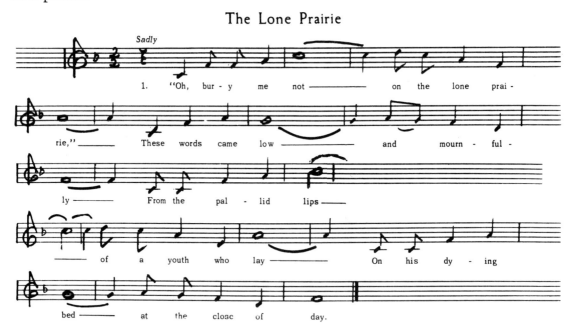

2. He'd wailed in pain until o'er his brow
   Death's shadows fast were gathering now.
   And he thought of home and his loved ones nigh
   As the cowboys came there to see him die.

3. "How oft I remember the well known words
   Of the free wild wind and the songs of birds,
   And I think of my cottage in the bower,
   And the friends I loved in my childhood's hour.

4. "And there is another who tears will shed
   For the one who lies in a prairie bed
   Oh, it pained me then and it pains me now,
   She has curled these locks and has kissed this brow.

5. "These locks she has curled, shall a rattler kiss?
   This brow she has stroked, shall a cold grave press?
   For the sake of those who will weep o'er me,
   Oh, bury me not on the lone prairie.

6. "Oh, bury me not on the lone prairie,
   Where wild coyotes will howl o'er me,
   Where the rattlers hiss, and the crow flies free,
   Oh, bury me not on the lone prairie."

When nearing the railroad corral at the end of the long, dusty trip up the trail, cowhands might have sung this joyful song.

The Railroad Corral

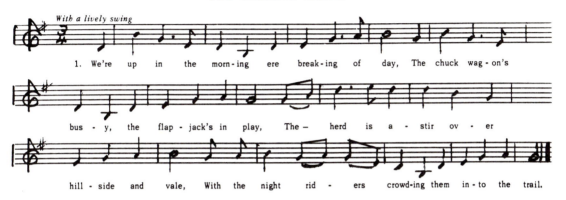

With a lively swing

1. We're up in the morn-ing ere break-ing of day, The chuck wag-on's bus-y, the flap-jack's in play, The herd is a-stir ov-er hill-side and vale, With the night rid-ers crowd-ing them in-to the trail.

3. The sun circles upward, the steers as they plod
   Are pounding to powder the hot prairie sod
   It seems, as the dust makes you dizzy and sick,
   That we'll never reach noon, and the cool shady creek.

6. But the longest of days must reach evening at last,
   The hills all climbed, the creeks all past.
   The tired herd droops in the yellow light;
   Let them loaf if they will, for the railroad's in sight.

A *Legendary Hero of the Cattle Country*

Opening up a huge area in which any state was larger than some two or three European countries was a job that needed thousands of rough, raw-boned, and carefree men who could live hard and work hard. These men came from everywhere. They rode the roundup, bedded cows down, and became American cowhands.

"Pecos Bill" and his horse, "Lightnin'," were to the cowhand what "Paul Bunyan" and "Babe, the Blue Ox" were to the lumbermen. Pecos Bill was the imaginative giant of the trail and range. It was said that as a baby he fell off a covered wagon. He was found and raised by the coyotes on the prairie. Many years passed and he was nearly a grown man before he discovered that he wasn't a coyote himself!

Many tall tales about Pecos Bill were told around the range and trail campfires. One told about the time his horse fell when Bill was riding at a gallop through a canyon. The fall broke the horse's neck and Bill had to hike on up the trail, carrying his beautiful silver saddle over his shoulder. Pretty soon he heard a noise coming from the cliff above him. Looking up, he saw two big, round eyes staring out from the brush. Quick as lightning a lithe form sprang out, whizzing through the air right on top of Bill. It was a big mountain lion as fierce as twenty wild-

"Pecos Bill" adapted from *Tall Tales from Texas* by Mody C. Boatright. Used by permission of the author.

cats. Bill wrestled him, throwing him this way and that, until the lion finally came meowing around as tame as any housecat. Then Bill flung his saddle on the lion. Whooping and yelling, he rode on up the canyon. Swinging his rattlesnake quirt, he made that big cat leap a hundred feet at a jump.

At last he came out in the open. He saw a chuck wagon and a bunch of cowboys eating around the campfire. Splitting the air with his war whoops, his lion screeching and spitting, Bill made his rattlesnake quirt sing as he rode up to the fire. Then he grabbed his lion by the ear, made him stop short, and slid from the saddle.

The cowboys just sat there speechless at such a sight. Spying a big pot of beans cooking over the fire, Bill reached in his hands, took out two sizzling fistfuls, and gulped them down,

red hot. Then he grabbed up the pot and drank all the boiling hot coffee. After that he said: "Who's the trail boss around here?"

A big fellow, eight feet tall, loaded with guns and bowie knives, stood up. He seemed kind of dazed as he spoke. "Stranger, I was, but now you can be."

The next day Bill set out, leading that bunch of cowhands. They ran down all the rustlers that had been sneaking around stealing cattle. They kept on until they had rounded up all the rustlers in the whole Southwest, so the cattle ranchers didn't ever again have to worry about having their cattle stolen.

Maybe you would like to find other tall tales told about Pecos Bill. You might like to write one, too.

As railroads were built and the long overland drives were no longer necessary, much wealth came to owners of the big herds. However, there were plenty of hardships. In the extremely cold winters many animals on the range froze to death. During years of drought when little rain fell to make grass grow, many cows died of starvation. During one of these times in the 1890's, some of the sons and grandchildren of William Wilson decided to move on westward into Arizona Territory.

One granddaughter of William Wilson had married Benjamin Stuart, grandson of the William Stuart who had pioneered Missouri. Benjamin Stuart had lost most of his fortune during the drought period. Perhaps because he had served as a United States Marshal and was a leader in many ways, it was he who organized the wagon train that was to go to Arizona Territory. The train was made up of family and friends who wanted to look for better grazing land farther to the West. Treasured possessions were loaded into wagons. Food for the six-month journey was carefully planned. One hundred extra head of horses were taken along by Benjamin Stuart because it was thought that settlers in the Arizona Territory would be anxious to buy them.

Some real life experiences of this pioneer family group might be interesting to you. For example, when the wagon train was several weeks on its way and many days ride on horseback beyond the end of the railroad, tragedy struck. The three-year old son of Benjamin Stuart was attempting to climb into the wagon driven by his grandmother. She didn't see that he was climbing up the wheel. When she started the horses, the wheel rolled around and right over his head.

150

At first, it was feared that he couldn't possibly live. In a desperate effort to help, a cowhand was sent as fast as his horse could carry him back to the railroad. From there he took the train to the nearest town where there was a doctor. After describing the accident to the doctor, the cowhand was told that there was nothing that could be done. He was given some worthless kind of medicine and sent back to tell the heartbroken parents. When he arrived back at the wagon train, the little boy was almost well! The soft bones of the skull, together with the tender handling of the people who knew how to face all kinds of problems and hardships, had saved the life of this child.

As the wagon train moved on, there were rest stops at springs or streams. Here the women did their laundry. Everyone bathed and put on clean clothes. This was almost like a family picnic, except that everyone, even the children, had definite chores to do. Some of the men were sent out to hunt for fresh meat almost every day.

Summer storms through the Southwest were a hazard. On one occasion, night caught up with the wagon train in a box canyon where "flash floods" sometimes came. On this particular night, thunder rolled and crashed through the canyon. During the flashes of lightning, the cowhands could see that the horses were

getting nervous and jumpy. There was no place for the wagons to go to be out of the way if the horses stampeded. Worse than that, it was feared that a cloudburst would send a flood down the canyon and wash everyone away.

When a tremendous clap of thunder finally "spooked" the horses, and they began to run, the cowhands were helpless to hold them. Fortunately for those in the wagon train, the horses ran in the opposite direction. But then it was not long until the roar of water could be heard. A flash flood did come roaring and frothing down the canyon. Again, fortunately, it did not strike the wagons with enough force to wash them away. Twice that night the lives of this westward-bound pioneer family group were spared.

Several days were spent in rounding up the stampeded horses! Then the wagon train moved on to an ultimate destination in southern Arizona Territory along the San Pedro River. Homes in this area were made of adobe bricks, and experienced Mexicans were hired to build houses for the new settlers. For a period of time, the life back in Texas was missed. Once again rude frontier life had to be endured. Schools and churches had to be built. There was the promise that it would be possible to return to Texas for a visit when the railroad was completed through to southern Arizona Territory. But by the time this happened, homesickness had been overcome. Arizona was now home. A new frontier had been settled.

To this frontier were brought the songs and dances of the Texas cattle country. Word often was sent around that there would be a picnic or a dance at one of the homes. After the school was built, it became the scene of most social events. "Box socials" were a popular kind of party. For this, each lady and young girl packed a very special lunch in a decorated box or basket. At the party, men and boys bid for the "box" that they wanted. Their dinner partner was the lady or girl to whom the box belonged. After the box dinners had been eaten, singing and dancing were enjoyed. There seemed always to be a fiddler who could play the tunes for square and round dances, schottisches, and two-steps. One of the favorite round dances was done to the tune of *Shoot the Buffalo.* Before you learn this dance you might like to think about the words of the verses. What do they mean to you?

Shoot the Buffalo

Liltingly

1. Rise you up, my dear-est dear, and pre-sent to me your hand, We are
roam-ing in suc-ces-sion to some far and dis-tant land, To some
far and dis-tant land, to some far and dis-tant land, We are
roam-ing in suc-ces-sion to some far and dis-tant land.

2. Oh, the buffalo is dead, for we shot him in the head;
We will rally round the cane-brake, and we'll shoot the buffalo.
And we'll shoot the buffalo, and we'll shoot the buffalo,
We will rally round the cane-brake, and we'll shoot the buffalo.

"Shoot the Buffalo" (song and dance directions) from *Music in Our Country,* copyright 1956, 1962, Silver Burdett Company. Used by permission.

The Dance

Formation: Double circle: boys inside, girls outside. *Dance:* First verse. Girls join hands and circle left; boys stand still, facing outward (4 measures). Each girl swings the boy facing her. End in double circle, boys outside facing counterclockwise; girls inside facing clockwise (4 measures). Grand right and left; All couples join right hands, walk past each other, giving left hand to the next, right hand to the following, etc., alternately. When original partners meet, girl takes boy's right arm and couples promenade counter-clockwise back to original places. (Repeat last 8 measures of song until this figure has been complete.)

Second verse. Boys join hands and circle left, while girls stand inside circle. Continue as above.

The children sing throughout the dance. The singing of the words will give direction to the dance if the words which end each phrase are kept in mind.

Over The Trail to Santa Fé

Santa Fé, in New Mexico, is one of the oldest cities in the United States. It was established by the Spanish in 1610. More than two hundred years later, in 1822, after William Becknell had sold his packtrain load of goods in Santa Fé for five times its worth, the first freight wagons made their way over the Santa Fé Trail from Arrow Rock, Missouri.

Other wagons soon followed.

Day after day, through deep dust or mud according to the weather, the wagons pulled by oxen, horses or mules moved slowly across the hot plains. When they reached the mountains and finally headed down the slopes toward Santa Fé, the wagon drivers began to dream of profits.

The arrival of a wagon train in Santa Fé created a great bustle of excitement among the people. *"Los Americanos!"* *"Los carros!"* and *"La entrade de la caravana!"* could be heard. People crowded around to see the newcomers.

Once in Santa Fé, the wagon drivers put on their best clothes and tied new "crackers" to their whips which they cracked loudly as they drove into the public square.

In this Spanish city American traders came face to face with a way of life that was strange to them. Santa Fé was a different world. Here people did not hurry. Most of them thought that politeness and gentility were more important than profits and ambition. The Mexican man's clothing was very gay with his *sombrero*, sash and *serape*. The women were equally as colorful in their dress. Life, on the surface, at least, was very gay and carefree. The men enjoyed such contests as horse racing and dog and cock fighting. Dancing to the music of fiddles and *bandolies* was an important part of their lives.

There was always much singing. Some of their songs were sad, while others were very gay. Many songs told love stories. Read the words to this song. What kind of song do you think it is?

Spanish Is the Loving Tongue

Gracefully
m p

1. Span - ish is the lov - ing tongue, Soft as mu - sic, light as spray;

'Twas a girl I learned it from, Liv - ing down So - no - ra way.

Though I've roamed this wide world o - ver, Yet I say her soft words o - ver,

Mi a - mor, mi cor - a - zon, Mi a - mor, mi cor - a - zon.

2. When she knew that I'd ride by,
She would listen for my spurs,
Open up her window wide,
Raise those laughing eyes of hers.
How my heart would nigh stop beating,
When I heard her tender greeting,
Whispered soft for me along,
Mi amor, mi corazon.

On the Santa Fé Trail

At first, only a few women braved the long, hot, dusty or muddy Santa Fé Trail. There was still danger of attack by Comanche Indians. However, it was not long before entire families began to use this route in their search for new homes in the Southwest. If you look at this picture carefully, you might discover many things about preparations that had to be made before wagon trains rolled out for Santa Fé.

One person who came to the Southwest over the Santa Fé Trail was Kit Carson. You may remember having read earlier that he was born in Kentucky and that he was taken to Boone's Lick in Missouri. In 1826, he ran away from the harness maker to whom he had been apprenticed by his mother. For the rest of his life, he lived in the Southwest.

Kit Carson became a legendary figure as a frontier scout. One elderly man said that, as a boy, he firmly believed Kit Carson to be at least ten feet tall, carrying a rifle so big that it required two ordinary men just to lift it. He imagined that Kit Carson drank out of nothing smaller than a river, and ate a whole buffalo as easily as a lady would eat the wing of a quail.

156

Ten years later, the man actually became acquainted with this famous frontiersman. He found Kit Carson to be just opposite of the way he had imagined him. He was a rather delicate, undersized, wiry man who was more quiet than boastful. When Kit Carson was shown an artist's sketch of himself with a huge rifle and many dead Indians, he wiped his glasses carefully and studied the drawing. He handed it back saying, "That might be me, but I sure don't recollect any such happening."

In this poem, you can read about some important events in Kit Carson's life:

KIT CARSON

On Christmas day in 1809, down South
Kentucky way,
Was born Kit Carson, great scout and mountain man,
Youngest of nine brothers.
The family moved to Missouri when Kit was a baby.
In the days of those pioneers
There were no public schools.
No books to learn about trades.
No railroads.
No electricity.
No telephones, radios, or television.
When Kit was a lad, he made saddles.
When he grew up, he joined a wagon train
To Santa Fé.
With his flintlock rifle flung over his back,
He trudged through the wilderness.
His bed was the earth.
His food—mush, molasses and buffalo meat.
From Santa Fé he went to Taos, New Mexico,
Where he learned Spanish from the Mexicans.
There he met a friend who promised to show
Him how to be a mountain man.
He wore a fringed, buckskin suit with a fur collar.
His sandy hair hung to his shoulders,
And on his head was a coonskin cap.
Kit Carson knew the Mohave and the Navajo,
The fierce Apache and the Crow,

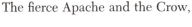

The Cheyenne, the Blackfoot, and the Arapaho.
He knew how to watch for an Indian ambush and the
Place of attack.
He knew how to handle fighting men!
He knew how to make a canoe and paddle it, too.
He knew how to keep his scalp.
Kit Carson joined John C. Fremont in 1843.
Across the wide Utah desert, over mountains,
And to northern California, they trekked—
The big wagons lumbering on and on!
In 1850, California became a state.
Kit Carson was chosen to ride to Washington, D.C.,
To give the news to the President.
Kit was given a lieutenant's commission.
Kit was made an Indian agent in New Mexico.
Kit knew how to make friends with Indians.
Kit learned the Indian language.
The Indians trusted him. They respected him.
Kit Carson said, "Let us learn to be brothers,
And to understand one another.
Let us dwell peacefully in this great and wonderful
Country—AMERICA!"

—Author Unknown

Blazing The Oregon Trail

From the very beginning of the wagon trail era in the 1830's, the Oregon Trail was the most important of the overland routes. It was also the longest wagon trail in history, stretching almost 2,000 miles through plains and mountains and deserts. This trail was blazed, or marked, when a party of seven was ordered to carry messages from the fur trading post at Astoria on the Pacific across country to New York.

The leader of this history-making brigade was Robert Stuart. Hardy, even-tempered and resourceful, the twenty-seven year old Scotsman was an ideal person to lead men on a dangerous assignment. Stuart kept a detailed diary in which he described the unusually large trees, rich soil, wildlife, and Indians.

After ten months of struggling through mountain passes and across deserts and plains, he and his men reached St. Louis on the Mississippi River. Their path was found later to be the one over which wagons could be taken. Robert Stuart lived until 1848 and saw the overland route he blazed become the great Oregon Trail.

Life On The Westward Trek to Oregon

The "jumping-off" places for the wave of settlers headed for Oregon were the Missouri River ports that were served by steamboat transportation. Wagon roads and trails led out from these supply towns and came together at Fort Kearney on the Platte River.

By 1843, the method of organizing a wagon train for the long journey West was well established. Some men even advertised in newspapers, inviting emigrants to meet and organize at certain outfitting towns on the western bank of the Missouri. Many experienced guides could be hired at these places. The month of May, when grass was high enough to provide food for the animals, was the usual starting time.

Families would come to the rendezvous, or starting place, with all their equipment. Each family had to have a sturdy, covered wagon, usually drawn by oxen, although horses and mules were sometimes used. They had to have

an adequate supply of flour, bacon, coffee, salt, dried fruit and molasses. Cooking utensils, tools, as well as firearms, gunpowder and lead were also needed. Cattle and extra oxen, horses or mules were driven beside the covered wagon.

At the rendezvous amidst the bawling of animals, the excited clamor of children, and dust stirred up by the wheels of wagons, the wagon-master or captain would take charge. The route was decided and a guide or scout hired. Only an imprudent or desperate family traveled alone. For protection against Indians, most trains consisted of about twenty-five to thirty wagons.

The story of everyday life on the trail has been told in diaries written by those who took part in this great adventure. At dawn, a bugle call would signal breakfast. Then the animals were rounded up and hitched to the wagons. At seven o'clock the day's journey began.

On to Oregon!   Los Angeles County Museum

As this picture shows, the wagons formed a single file as they spread out. Can you think of reasons why there might have been difficulty if wagons stayed grouped together?

After you have looked at the picture of a wagon train on page 161, read this poem. What does it tell you about life on the trail to Oregon? What information does it give you about the people after they reached their destination?

THE OREGON TRAIL (1843)

Two hundred wagons rolling out to Oregon,
Breaking through the gopher holes, lurching wide and free.
Crawling up the mountain pass, jolting, grumbling, rumbling on,
Two hundred wagons, rolling to the sun.
The women hold the guiding lines; beside the rocking steers,
With goad and ready rifle walk the bearded pioneers.
Through clouds of dust beneath the sun,
Through floods of sweeping rain,
Across Kansas prairie land,
Across Nebraska's plain.
Two hundred wagons, rolling out to Oregon,
Curved around the campfire flame at halt when day is done,
Rest awhile beneath the stars, yoke again and lumber on,
Two hundred wagons, rolling with the sun.
Now toils the dusty caravan with swinging wagon poles,
Where Walla Walla pours along,
Where broad Columbia rolls.
Then block the wheels, unyoke the steers; the prize is his who dares;
The cabins rise, the fields are sown, and Oregon is theirs!
They will take, they will hold,
By the spade in the mold,
By the seed in the soil,
By the sweat and the toil,
By the plow in the loam,
By the School and the Home!
Two hundred wagons, rolling out to Oregon,
Two hundred wagons, ranging free and far,
Two hundred wagons, rumbling, grumbling, rolling on,
Two hundred wagons, following a star.

—Arthur Guiterman

"The Oregon Trail (1843)" from *I Sing the Pioneer* by Arthur Guiterman. Copyright 1926, E. P. Dutton and Company, Inc., renewed 1954 by Mrs. Vida Lindo Guiterman. Reprinted by permission of the publishers.

On the trail, women and small children rode in the wagons while the men walked or rode horseback. Those who were on horses often acted as outriders, hunters and scouts, or took care of the loose livestock. A "nooning period" of four to five hours would divide a day. This allowed time for watering and grazing the animals, the noon meal, and a chance to rest during the hottest part of the day.

About three o'clock the wagon train started again and kept going until dusk. At night the wagons were "circled" and the animals kept close by. Inside the firelit circle the travelers would have their evening meal. They visited, told stories, sang songs and sometimes danced.

Almost always someone in the group could play the fiddle and call for square dancing. Some of the favorite tunes were *The Girl I Left Behind Me, Lady 'Round the Lady,* and *Buffalo Gals.* After you have learned these songs, you might enjoy doing the dance steps that go with them. Try to imagine that you are pioneers dancing inside the circle of wagons at night—with maybe Indians out there watching from the darkness!

The Girl I Left Behind Me

March time

1. I'm — lone-some since I crossed the hill And o'er the moor — and val - ley,

Such heav - y thoughts my heart do fill Since part - ing with my — Sal - ly.

I seek no more the fine and gay, For each does but re - mind me

How — swift the hours did pass a - way With the girl I left be - hind me.

2. The bee shall honey taste no more,
   The dashing waves shall cease to roar
   Ere she's to me a stranger.
   But now I'm bound to Brighton Camp,
   Kind heav'n may favor find me,
   And send me safely back again
   To the girl I left behind me.

"The Girl I Left Behind Me" from *This Is Music,* Book 5, by William R. Sur, Robert E. Nye, William R. Fisher, and Mary R. Tolbert. Copyright 1962, 1967, Allyn and Bacon, Inc. Used by permission.

A Square Dance

Formation: Four couples in a square. Head couple and 3rd couple face each other. The 2nd couple is on head couple's right, the 4th couple opposite. Girl of couple is always on the boy's right; corner girl is on his left. The position of each couple in this square is a permanent home to which couple always returns after circling, or a turn at executing a pattern.

1. Honor your partner. All square dances begin the same way, with a call, "Honor your partner." Partners face each other and bow. Then, "Honor your corner." All bow to the person on the other side.
2. Circling. The next call may be, "All join hands and circle left." Either a walking or skipping step may be used. This is followed by, "Circle right," upon which partners return to original place.
3. Buzz step. Boys take partners in regular dance position, holding girl at their right. This "Swing partners" is a whirl; partners keep right feet side by side, pushing with left foot.
4. "Promenade all." Form a double circle with boys on inside, facing counter-clockwise. Partner's hands are crossed as in skating position. Walk or skip around circle, ending in original position.

Lady 'Round the Lady

For it's La - dy 'round the La - dy and the Gent a - round the Gent

And the Gent a - round the La - dy and the La - dy 'round the Gent.

Four hands half, half right and left.

Swing your La - dy once a round and lead up to the next.

Buffalo Gals

Gaily

1. As I was wan-drin' down the street,
Down the street, down the street,
A pret-ty gal I chanced to meet,
Oh, she was fair to view.

REFRAIN

Then Buf-fa-lo gals, will you come out to-night,
Will you come out to-night, will you come out to-night,
Then Buf-fa-lo gals, will you come out to-night,
An' dance by the light of the moon?

2. I stopped her an' I had some talk,
   Had some talk, had some talk,
   Her foot covered up the whole sidewalk,
   An' left no room for me.

3. She's the prettiest gal I've seen in my life,
   Seen in my life, seen in my life,
   I wish very much she was my wife,
   Then we would part no more.

4. Oh make haste, Fan, don't make me wait,
   Make me wait, make me wait,
   I fear you've kept me now too late,
   Yes, there's the evening gun.

Wagon trains traveled about fourteen miles a day. The two-thousand mile trip required five months or longer, depending on the weather. The way was not easy. Disease and accidents caused many deaths. People were buried in crudely marked graves by the side of the trail.

River crossings were often hazardous. Some pioneers preferred to travel the last stretch of the trek to Oregon on the dangerous waters of the rivers. Log rafts were made on which travelers loaded the wagons and their possessions. Often lives were lost just before

people reached their desired destination.

Look at this picture and explain some of the things that could happen to people who tried to travel the Oregon rivers.

Traveling by Log Raft

Bureau of Public Roads

Those who lived through the trip remembered the good things about it. And despite the perils and hardships of wagon travel, many thousands of Americans reached Oregon in the 1840's. Even completion of the transcontinental railroad in 1869 did not put a stop to wagon travel. A man who went by train had to leave his team and wagon behind, and he needed both at whatever place he decided to stop to make his home. Arrival at the end of the trail did not mean the end of a covered wagon's usefulness. In it, crops and supplies continued to be hauled. Until the family could afford a surrey "with a fringe around the top," the wagon carried them to and from church, to picnics, and to the nearest town.

As on other frontiers, singing and dancing were favorite forms of entertainment. Dances were held in a home until public buildings were built. All the neighbors were invited. They danced and sang to such tunes as *Pop! Goes the Weasel!*

POP! GOES THE WEASEL!

POP! GOES THE WEASEL!

THE DANCE

Sets of three couples form about the room with about six feet of space between persons. The boys stand in one line and the girls in another. As they face the head of the room, the girls should be on the boys' right.

For each complete figuration of the dance, the music should be played or sung thus: Part A once, then Part B four times for the 4 "poppings" of the other members of the set by the head couple.

Part A

All around the chicken coop,	The head boy and girl each skip down the outside of their respective lines 4 skips.
The monkey chased the weasel. Monkey thought 'twas all in fun,	Now they skip back to their places—4 skips. They take 4 skips down the inside of the set with inside hands joined.
Pop! goes the weasel!	And back to place with 4 more skips and opposite hands joined.

Part B

I've no time to wait or sigh, No time to wheedle, Only time to say good-bye, Pop! goes the weasel!	Keeping the same hands joined, the head couple skips over to the girl of couple 2, joining their free hands with hers to form a small circle. They all skip to the L (clockwise) until the word "Pop!" On that word, the girl of the second couple is "popped" under the arch, made by the joined hands of the head couple, into her own place in the set.
Repeat Part B.	Now the head couple (without any break in their skipping) goes to the boy of couple 2, and circles with him and "pops" him into place.
Repeat Part B twice.	Then the girl of couple 3 and finally the boy are "popped", thus using up the music of Part B.

Couple 1 is now at the bottom of the set, so couple 2 becomes the new head couple and starts the dance from the beginning.

Couple 3 then has its turn, and the dance is over.

"Pop! Goes the Weasel!" (song and dance directions) from *Sing and Dance* by Beatrice A. Hunt and Harry Robert Wilson. Used by permission of the publishers, Schmitt, Hall and McCreary Company, Minneapolis, Minn.

Blazing the Mormon Trail

Oregon was not the only goal of pioneers who drove their wagons westward. Twelve hundred miles out from Independence, Missouri, where wagon trains were organized, the Oregon Trail forked. Settlers for Oregon went right; those who sought California or the Great Salt Lake Valley turned left.

In 1847, the Oregon Trail became a roadway of sorrow and hope for a particular religious group seeking a place where they could live in peace and safety. Known as the Church of Jesus Christ of Latter Day Saints, the members accepted, in addition to the Bible, the Book of Mormon. This consisted of sacred writings which their founder, Joseph Smith, said were revealed to him in a vision near Palmyra, New York.

The Mormons kept to themselves in practicing their faith. This made their neighbors suspicious and angry. In attempting to find a place far removed from unfriendly neighbors, the Mormons moved west, first to Ohio, then to Missouri, and finally to the Illinois frontier. But many other people wanted this rich Illinois prairie land, and before long the hard-working Mormons were again being harrassed and mistreated.

When Joseph Smith and his brother were killed in an outburst of violence in 1844, Brigham Young took command. In 1846, he and about two thousand of his followers moved across the Mississippi River and started a westward trek to a place near what is now Omaha, Nebraska. A steady stream of wagons were on the move. To provide for the near-destitute, Young had men plow the ground at each campsite. The next arrivals planted seeds; later ones weeded and irrigated; the late summer parties harvested the crops and transported them on to help supply food in winter quarters.

Brigham Young and his advisers read the reports of Lt. John Charles Fremont who had explored the Oregon Trail, the Great Salt Lake Valley, Oregon and California. Guided by these reports, Young decided where he would lead the Mormons. It was not to California or Oregon, but to the vast semi-desert valley of the Great Salt Lake. At the time, this area was not a part of the United States. It belonged to Mexico. Young thought that here, in what he would call his Kingdom of the Saints, the Mormons could live in peace and freedom.

In 1847, the first Mormon group, or "Pioneers" as they called themselves, moved out over the Oregon Trail. To avoid other emigrant parties, the group broke new ground that eventually became known as the Mormon Trail. Instead of following the south bank of the Platte River, as had earlier Oregon-bound settlers, the Mormons blazed a new road north of the river. To guide future Mormon groups, they even nailed signboards to poles alongside the road. Beyond the Green River, they took the left fork of the Oregon Trail.

At Fort Bridger, the trading post that Jim Bridger had established in 1842 on Blacks' Fork of the Green River, they rested for a few days. They were overjoyed to learn that it was only about one hundred miles farther to their destination. However, their joy faded as they found the desert trails ahead to be nearly impassable. Men and animals became exhausted. Many became ill. Even Brigham Young came down with the fever.

Then, on July 19, the great cliffs along the Weber River stopped them.

Men were sent in all directions to locate a trail. In the steep, rocky country it seemed impossible. But they worked, inspired by the knowledge that they were but a few miles away from their goal.

One day a report came back to Brigham Young, "We have opened a road through the canyon where it is uncertain whether man or beast ever trod before unless it be a bear or a rattlesnake."

Two days later, Brigham Young managed to sit up in his bed, lift the canvas wagon cover and look out over a broad, green valley. The Lake and the Great Salt flats stretched beyond as far as eye could see.

He said, "This is the place!"

Brigham Young and his Mormon followers were now a thousand miles from their enemies and they felt safe. However, when Mexico later ceded or signed over this land to the United States, the Mormons once again found themselves citizens of the United States. They endured many discouraging experiences. But, as it has been with other groups of people in this great land of ours who have worked hard and long and have been sincere in their beliefs, the Mormons eventually found peace and happiness.

Mormon Handcarts

You might like to know more about the famous Mormon Handcart Expedition —one of the later groups that traveled over the trail marked by Brigham Young's company. This expedition was made up of men and women who walked fifteen to twenty miles daily and pulled two-wheeled handcarts loaded with cherished belongings. Only babies and very young children rode. These people arrived in Salt Lake City on September 26, 1856, having traveled on foot across half a continent in three and one-half months.

What problems do you think these people had to solve as they traveled this long distance on foot?

There was a love for culture and beauty among the Mormons. They recognized the value of music. On the trail, each company had its brass and stringed instruments. When the day was over, tents pitched and supper finished, they gathered around the campfire, told stories, sang songs they loved, and often danced.

The words for the song, *Come, Come, Ye Saints*, was written by William Clayton to the tune of an old English song. This was done at Brigham Young's request while on the trail across the plains in 1847. It was used by every group that followed, to cheer the people and to help give them courage to continue the long, hard journey.

Come, Come, Ye Saints

With determination

1. Come, come, ye Saints, no toil nor la-bor fear; But with joy wend your way.

Though hard to you this jour-ney may ap-pear, Grace shall be as your day.

'Tis bet-ter far for us to strive, Out use-less cares from us to drive;

Do this, and joy your hearts will swell, All is well! All is well!

2. We'll find the place which God for us prepared,
   Far away in the West.
   Where none shall come to hurt or make afraid;
   There the Saints will be blessed.
   We'll make the air with music ring,
   Shout praises to our God and King;
   Above the rest these words we'll tell,
   All is well! All is well!

"Come, Come, Ye Saints" used by permission of the Corporation of the President of the Church of Jesus Christ of Latter-Day Saints.

A social hall for meetings and dances was completed in 1853 in Salt Lake City. While some churches forbade any form of dancing, the Mormons sponsored dances and looked upon dancing as a healthful exercise. Dancing was one of the fine arts that brought cheerfulness and joy into the hearts of the people. Their favorite dances included quadrilles or square dances, the Schottische, the Virginia Reel, polkas, and the Varsouvienne.

The Mormon pioneers had no need to make up stories. Their own every-day experiences have provided tales that have been told and retold for more than one hundred years. One such story tells how in 1855 a plague of grasshoppers, or locusts, appeared in the settlements of Utah and did much damage. They took all the crops and garden of a Grandfather Hemingway, except a tiny patch of garden peas. Each morning the grandmother would go to this patch and carefully pick every pea. This was about enough for one scant meal.

She would say, "I have picked every pea; these are the last. What will we do now"?

The grandfather would reply, "Have faith! We will be provided with enough food."

Each morning when she went to the patch, the grandmother would find just enough peas for one more meal. Each time she would say, "Now this is the last of them."

But when morning came, there would always be enough for another meal. This went on for weeks and actually kept the family alive.

There are many stories about the locust curse that threatened to destroy every living plant. This part of a poem written by Margaret Ball Dickson describes how the Mormon people feel about the thousands of sea gulls that appeared and saved their crops by eating the locusts.

So the "Garden of the Desert,"
Land of Utah, fair to see,
Wrote this law upon her tablets:
That there never more should be
Slaughter of a gull in Utah—
It should be a sacred bird.

The Mormon Legend of the Gulls

It was early spring, and in the fields the grain had sprouted early. A wonderful crop was in the making. Then in May, millions of large, black crickets, a type of locust, descended from the skies. They moved through the grain fields, eating every blade of grain in their path and leaving utter destruction behind them. The fields were left brown and bare.

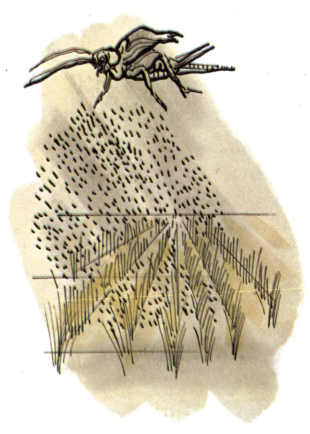

To try to save some of their fields, men, women, and children came and dug holes, burying the pests by the thousands. But there seemed to be as many left as ever. Ditches were plowed around the fields and water run through them in an effort to drown the locusts. But still more and more of them descended from the hills. Fire was tried with no better results. People were in despair.

Some said it was like trying to sweep back the rising tide of the ocean with a broom. And they knew that if they couldn't destroy this pest it meant starvation for settlers already in the Great Salt Lake Valley, as well as for the thousands of men, women, and children on their way there across the plains.

Then a miracle happened. The shrill, plaintive scream of sea gulls was heard from high in the sky. While the settlers watched in awe, the birds flew down and began to devour the locusts. More and more gulls came — thousands and thousands of the birds. To the stunned settlers these gulls were like angels from heaven. They would eat all they could, go to the stream to drink, regurgitate or throw up what they had eaten, and return to the fields to stuff themselves with more insects. And so it continued day after day until the locust plague was stopped. Many of the fields of the Mormon pioneers were saved.

Is it any wonder that the sea gulls became sacred in the thoughts of these early Utah settlers?

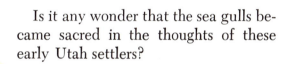

All Join In Stories, Games, and Riddles

Bits of old songs, sayings and riddles have been handed down for so long that they have become a part of the folklore of the world. Since the pioneers of Utah came from all parts of the civilized world, they brought with them the characteristics and expressions of their particular homelands. Some of the expressions have been so changed in repeating that they can be heard in several different ways. But it is the right of all people to change a saying to fit the situation.

When the pioneer girl complained about her features, the color of her eyes or hair, the mother or grandmother would say, "Handsome is as handsome does," or "Pretty is as pretty does." If the girl was too interested in clothes she might be told, "All is not gold that glitters."

Try to explain the meaning of each of these sayings:

. . . . . The mill can never grind with the water that has passed.
. . . . . It's foolish to lock the barn after the horse is stolen.
. . . . . School is a drill for the battle of life —
         if you fail in the drill, you will fail in the battle.
. . . . . It is better to wear out than rust out.
. . . . . Never find your delight in another's misfortunes.
. . . . . Empty cans make the most noise.

Parents and children in pioneer homes usually spent the evenings together around the fireplace. Riddles were told and games were played. Some of these were handed down from previous generations, while others were made up by the family. Are some of these riddles familiar to you?

. . . . What is taken from you before you get it?
. . . . Who was the fastest runner in the world?
. . . . Where are happiness and contentment
         always to be found?
. . . . Which is the strongest day of the seven?
. . . . What is good for a bald head?

About the only diversion for pioneer mothers was to visit friends and neighbors. When mothers went out for an afternoon, they had to take their children with them. Toys were scarce, so children learned to amuse themselves. The following are some games played by pioneer children. Have you ever played any of the same games?

Jolly Butcher Boy

The players choose-up sides. One team goes out and decides on the trade to be pantomimed. Then they stand facing the second team and say, "I'm a jolly butcher boy seeking a trade."

The others ask, "What can you do?"

The first team says, "Almost anything."

The others reply, "Show us your performance."

A pantomime is then performed which suggests some kind of work. If the correct guess is made, the performers run. If any of them are caught by the opposing side, they become members of that team. Then it is time for the second team to perform.

Pretty Bird in My Cup

The leader holds a tin cup of water in his hand as he walks around the inside of a circle of players. He thinks of a color, such as pink. Then he stops in front of one of the players and says, "Pretty bird in my cup, what color is yours?"

The player names a color. If it is not the one the leader has chosen, the leader passes to another player. But if the color named is the one thought of by the leader, he sprinkles water in the face of the player, and that player has to change places with the leader. The idea, of course, is to avoid guessing the right color.

Hide the Thimble

One player leaves the room while the group hides the thimble. The player is asked to return and find the thimble. If he is near it, the other players say, "Hot! Hot! Hot!" If he walks away from it, they say, "Cold! Cold! Cold!" In this way, he is guided until the thimble is found, then he gets to choose someone else to go out.

Pomp

This is a favorite outdoor game. A leader is chosen, usually by saying "Eenie, meenie, miney, mo," or some other counting rhyme. Two goal lines are made quite a distance apart. The leader stands on one goal line and the group at the other. The leader then calls, "Pomp, Pomp, pull away, run away, catch away!"

The players then make a dash for the leader's goal line. The leader—Pomp—tries to catch as many of the players as he can. Those he catches have to help him catch the others. The idea is to be the last player caught.

Early Arts and Crafts of the West

Most pioneers were so busy growing food and doing what they could to exist in a new land, that they had little time to think of beauty. But hardships could not completely destroy their longing for things to decorate their homes. There were some who practiced their art even as they traveled westward. Carl Christensen, a Dane from Copenhagen, came to Utah with one of the handcart companies in 1857. On the way he made many historical sketches of the Mormon people. A drawing similar to those made by Carl Christensen can be seen on page 172.

When pioneer artists could not buy paint, they made their own. Colored rocks were ground and mixed with oils, turpentines, and small amounts of wax to make a kind of smooth paint. Even bear grease and clay were sometimes used! Many times the color did not turn out to be the one that was wanted, but it was used anyway.

Pioneer art not only fulfilled a longing for decoration in the home; it supplied a practical need. Those most skilled in making things were called craftsmen. Many needlecrafts were practiced. Among the most popular were weaving, spinning, knitting, crocheting, netting, tatting, embroidery and cross-stitch handwork. You may want to find out more about each of these needlecrafts by looking in the encyclopedia. Perhaps you would like to try doing some of them.

Almost every home had a "motto" of greeting or inspiration, and a "sampler" of beautiful design and color on which a sentiment or historical fact was embroidered in cross-stitch handwork. These mottos and samplers were covered with glass and framed to give the effect of a picture. Perhaps in a museum you have seen a quilt or sampler that

has been handed down as an heirloom. Perhaps you have one in your own home.

One of the cherished decorations in the parlor or living room of the later pioneer homes was the glass globe. It would cover a colorful arrangement of waxed fruit, flowers made from wool, cotton or silk cloth, or sometimes natural flowers which had been treated for preservation.

The making of wax fruit like that under the glass globe in the illustration here became a popular hobby. Maybe you can find out how it was done. You might even like to try making some wax fruit.

Hat making, spinning, weaving and quilt making were other kinds of crafts that were practiced by women and girls in pioneer communities. Many women enjoyed designing patterns for quilts. Perhaps you would like to know more about this kind of art that provided covers for the beds, as well as beauty in the homes.

Quilt Making on the Western Frontier

Pioneer women were sometimes kept in their homes for weeks and months by snow and mud that made trails and roads impassable. During these times such "pickup" work as quilt-piecing was done. Between household chores, women planned and made quilts which might win the praise of neighbors.

It was part of the plan never to copy exactly a quilt made by another person. Each person tried to "top" her neighbor with a new variation of a geometric theme. Most of the designs were formed by arrangement of simple squares, diamonds and right-angled triangles. Only a few had curved seams because they were more difficult to make.

Part of the fun was the naming of a quilt. Sometimes the name chosen described the design. Often, though, the name selected was that of a person, place or historic event.

While the piecing was almost always done as pickup work by one woman whose hand stitching was nearly machine-perfect, the actual quilting was usually a group effort. Here was often an excuse for a party. When travel was finally possible, a group of neighbor women would gather together. Working diligently, they might complete the quilting of an entire top in one day. This meant that a thin layer of cotton was sewed between the quilt and a plain color backing. This sewing was done with small stitches that followed an all-over pattern.

A Square-Dance Party

National Life Insurance Company

In this picture, people seem to be enjoying the dancing that was almost always a part of the pioneer quilting party.

Combining work with pleasure, the "quilting bee" usually ended with a gay party in the evening. Then the men joined the group and food was served, usually in the form of a picnic spread. After everyone had eaten and visited, the fiddler struck up a dance tune. Here is one kind of dance that might have been enjoyed by people after a quilting bee. Can you "act out" the words?

Old Grumbler

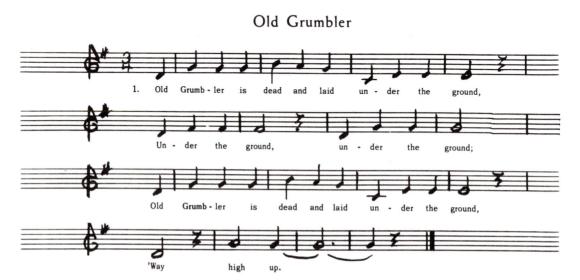

1. Old Grumbler is dead and laid under the ground,
Under the ground, under the ground;
Old Grumbler is dead and laid under the ground,
'Way high up.

2. His saddle and bridle lay under the shade.
3. There stood an old apple tree over his head.
4. The apples were ripe and ready to drop.
5. There came an old lady a-picking them up.
6. Old Grumbler he rose and he gave her a knock.
7. That made the old lady go hippety-hop.
8. She hippety-hopped to Strawberry Hill.
9. And there she sat down and made her will.
10. If you want any more, you'll sing it yourself.

"Old Grumbler" from *New Music Horizons*, Fourth Book, copyright 1945, 1953, Silver Burdett Company. Used by permission.

After the dancing, visitors gathered their belongings, loaded their wagons, and started for home. What does this folk song tell about a quilting party?

Aunt Dinah's Quilting Party

Leisurely

1. In the sky the bright stars glit - tered, — On the bank the pale moon shone; And 'twas from Aunt Di - nah's quilt-ing par - ty

1-2. I was see - ing Nel - lie home. I was see - ing Nel - lie home, I was see - ing Nel - lie home, And 'twas from Aunt Di - nah's quilt - ing par - ty I was see - ing Nel - lie home.

2. On my arm a soft hand rested,
   Rested light as ocean foam;
   And 'twas from Aunt Dinah's quilting party

Pioneer Furniture

Pioneers of the West did not allow their hard struggle for existence to destroy their love for fine things. "Back East" many of these people had lived in beautifully furnished homes. A few were able to bring some of their most cherished pieces with them. However, the covered wagon was not large enough to carry many things. There were even heart-breaking times when the load had to be lightened and fine furniture left by the side of the trail.

These same people, when they reached their destination, made rough-hewn tables, chairs, cupboards, beds and chests from such wood as they could find. Sometimes they had to haul suitable wood from distant mountain canyons. They learned to make their own glue, pegs, paints, stains and colorings.

Much of the furniture used by the pioneers showed evidence that even the earliest settlers strove to add beauty and refinement to their homes. The most ordinary kinds of soft woods were beautifully carved and stained.

Below is a picture showing furniture in a pioneer girl's room. Compare it with a girl's room today.

Los Angeles County Museum

As railroads pushed westward, freight trains brought choice pieces of furniture such as stoves, sewing machines, organs and pianos from eastern markets. Only the well-to-do or the most thrifty could afford such luxuries. In nearly every pioneer museum can be found a few of these precious pieces. Many museums will have melodeons on display. Perhaps you can find out how a melodeon is different from a piano.

Western Wagons

They went with axe and rifle, when the trail was still to blaze,
They went with wife and children, in the prairie-schooner days.
With banjo and with frying-pan — Susanna, don't you cry.
For I'm off to California to get rich out there or die!

We've broken land and cleared it, but we're tired of where we are.
They say that wild Nebraska is a better place by far.
There's gold in far Wyoming, there's black earth in Ioway,
So pack up the kids and blankets, for we're moving out today.

The cowards never started and the weak died on the road.
And all across the continent the endless campfires glowed.
We've taken land and settled — but a traveler passed by,
And we're going West tomorrow — Lordy, never ask us why!

We're going West tomorrow, where the promises can't fail
O'er the hills in legions, boys, and crowd the dusty trail!
We shall starve and freeze and suffer, we shall die and tame the lands.
But we're going West tomorrow, with our fortune in our hands.

—Rosemary and Stephen Vincent Benét

"Western Wagons" by Rosemary and Stephen Vincent Benét from *A Book of Americans* published by Holt, Rinehart and Winston, Inc, copyright 1933 by Rosemary and Stephen Vincent Benét, renewed 1961 by Rosemary Carr Benét. Reprinted by permission of Brandt and Brandt, Literary Agents.

Gold!

Gold in the American River!

Gold at the grassroots! Gold *everywhere!* Pick it up while staking out your horse . . .

By late summer of 1848, when news about the discovery of gold in California reached the East, the "yellow fever," or gold craze, broke out in much of Europe and in some parts of Asia as well as all over the United States. It seemed as if *everyone* was either already on the way or getting ready to start to California.

Gold seekers from the Atlantic States usually went by ship. Those from the Mississippi basin took the land routes.

Southerners naturally followed southern routes through El Paso or Santa Fé. Others took the northern route over the Sierra Nevada. They filled the trails in wagons, on horses, behind pushcarts, and on foot. In their rush to get there, they didn't organize themselves as the Oregon pioneers did, and when a man traveled alone, he sometimes ran into difficulties since there was no one to help him.

One Man's Dream

This is a true story about a young man named William Stuart who started to California from Missouri. He was so anxious to get there to find his share of gold that he cut across country from his home in Missouri, hoping to find the Oregon Trail. After he had traveled several days with no settlements in sight, he became ill. His fever was so high that he was delirious. He couldn't even stand up, so of course he couldn't saddle his horse or ride. He was in this condition for three days, but his horse and his little dog stayed close to him.

Finally, his fever "broke" and he became conscious of where he was. He was too weak to get up, however. He did manage to drink water from his canteen and eat some dried meat. After two more days, he was able to saddle his horse and ride. He found the Oregon Trail and "joined up" with others who were headed for California. Among these people was the famous frontier scout, Jim Bridger.

The people with Bridger were headed for the gold fields. They were a gay, carefree kind of people who sang and joked as they rode along the trail. The song, *Whoa! Ha! Buck and Jerry Boy* might have been one of the songs they sang. The third verse tells you that the dirty, dusty trail was forgotten at night when the dancing began. Who do you think Buck and Jerry Boy are?

Whoa! Ha! Buck and Jerry Boy

1. With a mer-ry lit-tle jog and a gay lit-tle song, Whoa! Ha! Buck and
   We trudge our way the whole day long, Whoa! Ha! Buck and
   Jer-ry Boy, jer-ry Boy.
   What though we're cov-ered all o-ver with dust, It's
   reach Salt Lake some day or bust,
   bet-ter than stay-ing back home to rust, We'll
   (Spoken)
   Whoa! Ha! Buck and Jer-ry Boy.

2. There's a pretty little girl in the outfit
      Whoa! Ha! Buck and Jerry Boy,
   I wish she was by my side instead,
      Whoa! Ha! Buck and Jerry Boy,
   Look at her now with a pout on her lips,
   As daintily with her fingertips,
   She picks for the fire some buffalo chips.
      Whoa! Ha! Buck and Jerry Boy.

3. O tonight we'll dance by the light of the moon,
      Whoa! Ha! Buck and Jerry Boy,
   To the fiddler's best and only tune,
      Whoa! Ha! Buck and Jerry Boy,
   What though we're covered all over with dust,
   It's better than staying back home to rust,
   We'll reach Salt Lake some day or bust!
      Whoa! Ha! Buck and Jerry Boy.

Another favorite song of the gold-seekers was *Sweet Betsy from Pike.* What story does this song tell?

Sweet Betsy from Pike

1. Oh, don't you re-mem-ber sweet Bet-sy from Pike,
Who crossed o'er the moun-tains with her hus-band Ike,
With two yoke of ox-en, a big yel-low dog,
A tall Shang-hai roost-er and one spot-ted hog?

REFRAIN

Too-ra lee————, too-ra-lay————,
Sing-ing too-ra-lee, too-ra-lee, too-ra-lee-ay.

2. One evening, quite early, they camped on the Platte,
Twas near by the road on a green shady flat.
Poor Betsy, sorefooted, lay down to repose,
In wonder Ike gazed on his Pike County rose.
Refrain

3. Their wagon broke down with a terrible crash,
And out on the prairie rolled all kinds of trash.
Poor Ike got discouraged, and Betsy got mad;
The dog drooped his tail, and looked wondrously sad.
Refrain

4. They soon reached the desert where Betsy gave out,
And down in the sand she lay rolling about,
And Ike, half distracted, looked down in surprise,
Saying, "Betsy, get up, you'll get sand in your eyes."
Refrain

5. Then Betsy got up with a great deal of pain,
And said she'd go back to Pike County again,
But Ike heaved a sigh, and they fondly embraced,
And they traveled along with his arm 'round her waist.
Refrain

"Sweet Betsy from Pike" from *This Is Music*, Book 5, by William R. Sur, Robert E. Nye, William R. Fisher, and Mary R. Tolbert. Copyright 1962, 1967, Allyn and Bacon, Inc. Used by permission.

William Stuart went with Jim Bridger to the gold fields. After finding that a fortune in gold could not be had as easily and as quickly as he had thought, he decided to return to Missouri. Stuart, one other person and Jim Bridger set out to follow the southern route to Santa Fé. As they were swimming their horses across the Colorado River, they were attacked by Indians. William Stuart and Jim Bridger reached the opposite side of the river safely, but Bridger had an arrow in his leg above the knee. He cut the shaft off the arrow and rode for several days before reaching Santa Fé where there was a doctor who could remove the part of the arrow that was still in his leg.

William Stuart parted from Bridger and followed the Santa Fé Trail on to Missouri. Once back home, he married the girl who was waiting for him. Together they made plans to go to California to live. Before they could do this, however, the Civil War started, and William Stuart had to leave his wife and two little boys while he served as a scout for the Southern, or Confederate, Army.

As Captain Bill Stuart, he went through enemy lines on many daring raids. He was captured once but quickly escaped from prison and rejoined his company. Because he was known to be a very successful spy for the South, orders were issued from the Union Army to recapture him.

After the war was over, when he should have been safe, enemy soldiers surrounded his home. They called him outside and took him away into the woods where they shot him. This left his wife and two young sons to care for themselves. The dream of going to live in California ended for William Stuart's wife because her thoughts were now directed toward making a living for her two sons.

With the courage of most pioneer women, she faced her problems squarely and succeeded over the years in guiding her sons into profitable cattle ranching in Texas. You will remember reading earlier about one of these sons. He was the Benjamin Stuart who, after a number of drought or dry years in the 1890's, organized a wagon train of relatives and friends and headed west into Arizona Territory in search of new cattle-grazing land.

Westward to the Pacific

After about twenty years of living in Arizona, Benjamin Stuart moved his own family on to California. This completed the story of the coast-to-coast westward migration of a particular American family—a migration that took more than one hundred years.

Perhaps this is the time to tell you about the last part of the migration—from Arizona to California. Remember that, because there were no railroads, the family traveled to the Arizona Territory by wagon train. During the twenty-year period that the family had lived in Arizona, a railroad was built through their area and on into California. When they moved to California, the journey was made by train. They stayed in the Imperial Valley for a few months, then decided to buy a cattle ranch in the San Joaquin Valley near Tulare.

By this time, in 1915, many people owned automobiles. Benjamin Stuart bought a Dodge car shortly before taking his family on the last lap of their westward journey. It should be explained here that a cattleman who had spent many years in the saddle often had a hard time getting used to driving an automobile. When in a tight place, instead of stepping on the brake to stop, he was apt to pull back on the steering wheel and yell, "Whoa!"

The Stuart family had many adventures while traveling by automobile to the San Joaquin Valley. One of the most harrowing occurred when they had to go up a steep and narrow mountain road in the rain. Of course, most of the roads at that time were not paved. When it rained, the roads were very slippery and muddy.

After slipping and sliding from side to side and almost over the embankment into the deep canyon below, they finally reached what seemed to be the top of the mountain. There they ran into a road detour sign stating "Bridge Out! Return to the bottom of the mountain grade and take alternate route."

By this time, the mother wanted to get out and walk. The children were crying and begging their father to take them home. For safety's sake, he had the family get out of the car.

The cliff edge went straight down. There was barely enough room for the car on the road, and it seemed impossible to turn around. The brakes on cars of that day weren't too dependable either! But by backing and pulling forward a few inches at a time, and doing this over and over again, he was finally able to turn the car around. The trip down the mountain was worse than the way up, but they made it, and finally reached the ocean—the first time for the children to see the great Pacific! As they traveled across long bridges over back bays and rivers, they stared in wonder at so much water. When asked later if they had seen the ocean, they replied, "Oh, yes! We crossed it a lot of times!"

When they reached Santa Ana, California, they decided to stop at a hotel until the weather was better. It was raining steadily. The four children became too noisy in the hotel room, because they hadn't had a chance to play during their long ride. To keep them quiet, the oldest boy was told to take them to the "flickers," as movies were called at that time. This was another exciting adventure, because it was the first time the children had seen moving pictures.

After two days, the family resumed the journey. When they reached Newhall, they were told that the Ridge Route over the mountains was closed due to the storm. Benjamin Stuart had never let such things as muddy roads keep him from going where he wanted to go. He put chains on the car wheels and proceeded.

Today the Ridge Route between Los Angeles and Bakersfield is a wonderful, wide freeway. But in 1915, it was a winding, steep and dangerous dirt road. During storms, parts of the road were often washed away. There were many dangerous earth and rock slides. For an inexperienced driver, it was a perilous road to attempt even in good weather.

However, people who had followed the pioneer trails to live on the frontier were used to overcoming dangerous obstacles, so it was not surprising that

Benjamin Stuart decided to go on over the mountains. Mrs. Stuart and the children gradually overcame their fear of mountain roads and began to look upon this part of the journey as an exciting adventure.

Midway on the mountain road, they came upon a lone man and his little red

roadster, which was stuck in the mud. After trying to help the man start his "sports-car," he was offered a ride to the next place where he could obtain help. He piled into the already crowded Stuart car and they all proceeded along the dangerous route until Lebec was reached, where they left the stranger at a garage.

The family found a cabin to rent where they spent the night. This cabin was not like a motel room where travelers stay now. Instead, it was one of several bare, roadside cabins. Travelers had to carry their own blankets with them and provide their own food.

Later, cabins were built together and called "auto courts" because there was usually a place beside each cabin for an automobile to be parked. Auto courts and "tourist camps" gave way to motels, where services are provided similar to those at hotels.

The San Joaquin Valley ranch was reached late the next day. There was excitement in exploring the new home and surroundings before dark. The large ranch house had not been lived in for several months. Although it had been cleaned and prepared for the family's arrival, there was an air of spookiness about the rooms. This was made worse by the fact that the furniture, which had been shipped by freight train, had not arrived.

The Stuart family slept that night on pallets made by putting blankets on the floor. When everyone was "bedded-down" the house became very quiet.

"Creaking" began as the night air cooled the wood and caused it to contract. Between creaks, strange "ghost sounds" were heard. No one slept a great deal. Even the father began to wonder what kind of place this was. It sounded as if the house were being bombarded by small rocks that hit the roof and rolled slowly off. Yet when he went out to investigate, he could see nothing in the dark.

The mystery was solved when morning came. It was discovered that a large oak tree which shaded the house was dropping its acorns or seeds. As each acorn hit the roof, it sounded like a small rock. This kind of tree was new to the family. Oak trees had not grown where they lived in Arizona or in the Imperial Valley in California. The children grew to love this beautiful tree with its wide-spread branches that were so good for climbing.

The Stuart family gradually became settled in this new home in the central part of the San Joaquin Valley in California. This was as far West as they planned to go —at least, for the time being.

Wagon Trails West Activities

1. Make a large map showing the main trails west. Draw pictures of the ways people traveled. Show the rest-stops at forts.

2. Make a model of old Santa Fé with adobe buildings, Mexicans in their native dress, *carretas* pulled by oxen, and the mule trains that first packed supplies between California and Santa Fé.

3. Find additional Mexican folk songs that might have been sung in old Santa Fé.

4. Make a model of a particular Indian tribe's camp. Give information about tribal rule. Give the name of the chief.

5. Collect pictures and information about early guns. Share this information with your class.

6. Suppose it is the year 1844, and that your family is getting ready to join a wagon train headed for California. What supplies would you take with you? Where would you look for information to help you? Give good reasons for the selection of each item on your list. If your list is too long, and the weight of the items totals more than is allowed, which things should be left behind? Be ready to defend your decisions to the class, because they might disagree with you.

7. Plan a square dance party for a wagon train stop. What information would you need? Perhaps the class can learn songs and dances to present in a program for parents.

8. Pretend that you are in charge of a wagon train. Make a list of your duties. Present your list before the class. Other pupils will challenge you if you have failed to list all of your responsibilities.

9. Find out what part boys and girls took in the long overland trips to the West. Certainly they didn't just ride and look at the scenery for days and days. Look in books and use your imagination, too. Pretend that you have just reached Oregon in 1846, and write a letter for a trader to take back to a friend in Ohio. Tell what you had to do on the trip—what you liked and what you disliked about the journey.

10. Find out more about the grasshopper and cricket plagues in Utah. Share this information with the class.

11. Look in an encyclopedia for information about how a beautiful temple was built by the Mormons in Salt Lake City. Be sure to include in the report the story about where they obtained the wood for the great pipe organ that was made for the temple.

12. Design some quilt patterns. Perhaps each girl in the class might sew a quilt block. Then all of the blocks could be put together to make a quilt top.

13. Make a scrapbook of pioneer games, riddles and wise sayings. Draw pictures to illustrate some of the things in the scrapbook.

14. Design a greeting or a sampler to be made with cross-stitching. Where can you find information about how to do this?

15. Pretend that you are an artist for an Eastern newspaper. You are supposed to send back news of what is happening in California. Draw a series of pictures of a wagon train arriving in Sacramento during gold rush days. Some of the pictures might be quite humorous.

16. "Gold" was the magic word that started the rush to California in 1849. Would you want a gold rush to take place in your community? Make a list of the advantages and disadvantages as you see them, and hold a class discussion. At the end of the discussion, take a vote to see what the general opinion is.

What interesting information can you get from reading this poster advertisement from one of the early travel lines?

CHAPTER IV

OTHER WAYS OF TRAVELING WEST

Stagecoach

The many people who went to Oregon in the 1840's, as well as the rush of gold seekers to California in 1849, created a need for overland passenger service. People began to demand something more comfortable and convenient than wagons and pack horses. Although the West was someday to have transcontinental railroads, stagecoach passenger service filled in until that time came.

There were many types of stagecoaches, but the most famous was the Concord coach. This stage was designed to provide some comfort for passengers and to withstand the abuse it had to take on the rough western roads.

The most important person in western stagecoach travel was the driver. His hands had to control six spirited horses when they took the rocky roads at a fast gallop. He was responsible for the comfort and safety of his passengers; he collected the tickets, and tried to keep to a fixed schedule from one station to the next, usually a distance of from ten to twenty miles.

A stage station was usually located in a town's best hotel. Travel schedules called for early morning departures, and passengers had to be awakened in time for breakfast. An important passenger was usually given a place of honor with the driver on the high "box" seat. If money or gold was carried, the services of a "shotgun messenger," or guard, was required. In this case, the important person was given his choice of inside seats.

Out on the road, the pace of the horses was a gallop except where hills and curves might slow the pace to a walk or a gentle trot. The average speed, however, was not high—about five miles per hour.

There were many stops, because teams had to be changed at every station. Drivers were relieved at the end of the day. The journey was a tiring one for passengers, and those who wished to break up the trip could find a place to stay at some of the stations. It was quite common for passengers reaching their destinations to take a good bath, get a full night's sleep, and have nothing more to do with stagecoaches—at least for a while.

Stagecoach travel was not exactly safe! Nor was it dull. Teams sometimes ran away, causing upsets and breakdowns. When a coach got stuck in the mud, the passengers had to get out to lighten the load. Often they had to help push the coach through the boggy spot. Indian attacks were frequent through 1865 on the central route. Stagecoach holdups were always a possibility in the Rocky Mountains, Black Hills, and Pacific Coast regions where mines were located and where passengers carried large sums of money.

A Great American Legend

Man has always been in a hurry to get where he wants to go, and, once there, is often in just as big a rush to get the news from the place he left. In the western part of our country, it was no different. The settlers had traveled as fast as they were able to the free land and new homes. The gold seekers had come and spread rapidly across the hills and valleys. Merchants, lumbermen and stockmen followed, and no sooner had they reached their destination than they became anxious for word and goods from home.

This demand for speed and for uniting East with West brought the stagecoachers and expressmen. It started the nation stringing telegraph wires and driving railroad spikes. The Pony Express, which consisted of a pony relay line that provided ten-day mail service between the Missouri River and Sacramento, was doomed from the beginning. Completion of the first transcontinental telegraph line in October of 1861 brought with it the end of the Pony Express. But though the riders, their horses, the mail pouches and most of the way stations are gone now, they have become a special part of a great American legend.

Mark Twain described the Pony Express riders this way:

"Here he comes!"

Every neck is stretched farther and every eye strained wider. Away across the endless dead level of the prairie a black speck appears against the sky, and it is plain that it moves. Well, I should think so! In a second or two it becomes a horse and rider, rising and falling, rising and falling — sweeping toward us nearer and nearer — growing more and more distinct, more and more sharply defined — nearer and nearer, and the flutter of hoofs comes faintly to ear — another instant a whoop and a hurrah from our upperdeck, a wave of the rider's hand, but no reply, and man and horse burst past our excited faces, and go winging away like a belated fragment of a storm!

So sudden is it all, and so like a flash of unreal fancy, that but for the flake of white foam left quivering and perishing on a mailsack after the vision had flashed by and disappeared, we might have doubted whether we had seen an actual horse and man at all, maybe.

Excerpt from *Roughing It* by Mark Twain. Published by Harper and Row, Publishers.

A Pony Express Rider

Bureau of Public Roads

A Windwagon

Harnessing the Wind for Faster Travel

"Harness the wind and reap the whirlwind" was an appropriate proverb to describe one of the most unusual means of transportation in the history of the West. Impatient to reach their destination, some travelers and gold seekers experimented with faster transportation. One answer to the problem was the sail-equipped, wind-powered wagon. Many jokes and stories were told about this strange vehicle. Among the famous stories is that of Windwagon Thomas, an ex-sailor who arrived in Westport Landing, now Kansas City, on the Missouri River one day in 1853.

The sailor had his own small vehicle, and what he thought was a wonderful plan. He proposed to carry passengers and freight rapidly across the plains in wind-driven wagons. He demonstrated in his own strange vehicle to prove that this could be done. A group of businessmen pooled their money and a huge wagon was built. It was twenty-five feet long and seven feet wide, with wheels twelve feet in diameter. Its two masts were rigged with large sails.

Windwagon Thomas himself decided to take the group of men for their first ride. The wagon, after sailing wildly around in circles for over an hour, finally ended smashed against a rancher's fence. The men said they would have nothing more to do with this "contraption." Windwagon Thomas picked himself up and sailed away in the one-man wagon which had brought him there. He was never seen again.

How do you know, by looking at the photograph on page 204, that people were curious to know whether the windwagon would work?

Smoked Out

The "iron horse" that spanned the prairie
And expedited fetch and carry;
Which metamorphosed into metal
That swallowed distance in its flight
A mile a minute through the night;
Which turned an 18th century dream
Into the mighty age of steam,
Will soon retire to rust from traction
No longer panting hot for action . . . .
The iron horse worked hard to please all
And won all starts till came the diesel.

—Charles S. Adelman

"Smoked Out" by Charles S. Adelman from *Rhymes and Remnants* in The Chicago Tribune.

Westward Travel by Train

By 1857, it was possible to travel by rail from the Atlantic Ocean to St. Louis, Missouri. Rail service reached across Missouri by 1865. Then, work by different kinds of people, including Irish, Negro and Chinese laborers, laid railroad tracks from the West coast to meet those from the East. Within three years the two great oceans were joined by a transcontinental railroad.

Sometimes the railroad workers sang as they worked. Singing helped them to keep a steady rhythm while putting greater force into their hammer strokes. Songs like *This Ol' Hammer* were called railroad work songs.

This Ol' Hammer

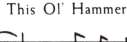

1. This ol' ham-mer, —— (uh!) Jump-in' ham-mer, —— (uh!) This ol' ham-mer, —— (uh!) Driv-in' ham-mer, —— (uh!) This ol' ham-mer, —— (uh!) Mean ol' ham-mer, —— (uh!) Killed poor John, —— but it won't kill me.

2. Night is fallin' – (uh!)
All around us, – (uh!)
Night is fallin' – (uh!)
All around us, – (uh!)
Night is fallin' – (uh!)
All around us, – (uh!)
Ain't no restin' till the judgment day.

3. Boss man's comin', – (uh!)
Hear him runnin', – (uh!)
Boss man's comin', – (uh!)
Hear him runnin', – (uh!)
Boss man's comin', – (uh!)
Hear him runnin', – (uh!)
Boss man's comin', but he won't find me.

"This Ol' Hammer" from *Voices of America* by Wolfe, Krone, and Fullerton. Follett Publishing Company, copyright 1963.

John Henry is a legendary hero whose fabulous strength was celebrated by working men, first in the South and later all over the country. He worked on the longest and most difficult tunnel that man had ever cut through a mountain. Sing *John Henry* and discuss its story with your classmates.

John Henry

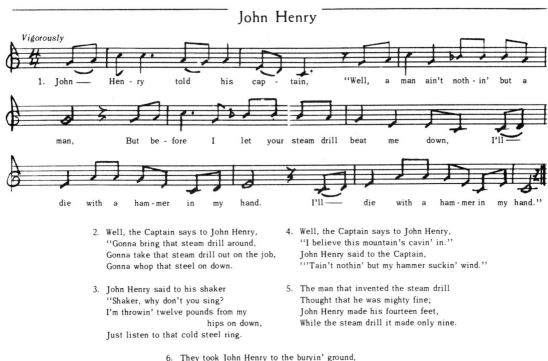

Vigorously

1. John — Hen - ry told his cap - tain, "Well, a man ain't noth - in' but a man, But be - fore I let your steam drill beat me down, I'll — die with a ham - mer in my hand. I'll — die with a ham - mer in my hand."

2. Well, the Captain says to John Henry,
   "Gonna bring that steam drill around,
   Gonna take that steam drill out on the job,
   Gonna whop that steel on down.

3. John Henry said to his shaker
   "Shaker, why don't you sing?
   I'm throwin' twelve pounds from my
                              hips on down,
   Just listen to that cold steel ring.

4. Well, the Captain says to John Henry,
   "I believe this mountain's cavin' in."
   John Henry said to the Captain,
   "'Tain't nothin' but my hammer suckin' wind."

5. The man that invented the steam drill
   Thought that he was mighty fine;
   John Henry made his fourteen feet,
   While the steam drill it made only nine.

6. They took John Henry to the buryin' ground,
   And they buried him in the sand;
   And every locomotive come roarin' round
   Says, "There lies a steel-drivin' man."

"John Henry" from *Music in Our Country*, copyright 1956, 1962, Silver Burdett Company. Used by permission.

Most Indians feared the advance of the railroads. Look at this picture. What thoughts do you think the Indians have as they watch the "iron horse" move over the plains?

The "Iron Horse"   *Association of American Railroads*

An Early Club Car

Railroads greatly increased the number of people who traveled to the West. The traveler at one time had to be content with a thorough jolting in a Concord stage and with unsatisfactory meals at rough, untidy stations. With the coming of the railroad, it was possible to travel in luxury.

Some trains had newly invented sleeping coaches called "Pullmans" and "Silver Palace Cars." These cars were richly appointed with beds and private toilet facilities. For those who couldn't afford such luxury, there were unreserved coach accommodations.

To attract the patronage of recently arrived emigrants from Europe, there was the emigrant car—plain but equipped with a toilet, a coal-burning pot-bellied stove, hard seats, and bunks with straw-filled bags for mattresses.

Dining cars and trackside eating places were available to all. Both offered foods of a quality never before known to travelers in the West.

Emigrants Association of American Railroads

Winter slowed but didn't stop "the cars." Trains crept through wooden sheds under the snows that had sometimes buried wagon and horse travelers.

Perhaps you know the tragic story of the Donner party. Their wagons arrived too late in the year to make the mountain crossing. They tried. They were buried in snow and many starved to death. Their route over the high Sierra Nevada came to be known as the Donner Pass Route. When a railroad was built to follow this route, sheds were constructed over the tracks to keep the heavy snows from burying them. These sheds had to be inspected every few hours for "cave-ins."

A true story of one man's experience while serving as a "snow shed inspector" on the Donner Pass illustrates again the bravery and resourcefulness of our pioneers:

Sierra Snowsheds Association of American Railroads

Uncle Dickie Benton and the Mountain Lion

From Missouri to the gold fields of California had come a man in search of adventure and wealth. When he learned that someone was needed to spend the winter atop Donner Pass to inspect the snow sheds and help keep the railroad open, he volunteered for the job. He knew that it would be a long, lonely time, but he was pleased by this opportunity to work for the railroad company.

Days and weeks passed and the snow grew deeper and deeper. As he walked through the long, dark snowshed tunnels looking for places that might not stand the weight of more snow, he began to think that he was being watched and followed.

At first he thought it was his imagination because he had been alone for such a long time. Then one day he came upon fresh tracks of a mountain lion. After that, he remained alert to danger from the time he left his cabin until he returned. Although he could sense the near-presence of the lion, he could never catch sight of him. This went on until he began to feel that he and the lion were matching wits. He wondered if the lion might suddenly, around some curve or dark place, become the victor in this contest.

Then one night Uncle Dickie was awakened from sleep by the tearing of shakes or shingles from the cabin roof. The lion was trying to reach him, perhaps because other food had been impossible to find.

Uncle Dickie did some fast thinking. If he fired a shot through the roof and merely wounded the lion, his danger would become even greater. A wounded animal becomes increasingly desperate for food, since, in most cases, it is unable to run down or catch other animals.

Uncle Dickie thought some more. If he waited and the lion weakened the shakes to the point that he crashed through the roof, what then? The lion might kill with one rake of his claws before he could be shot.

Finally Uncle Dickie decided to risk firing through the roof. He lifted his rifle and aimed at a spot behind the sound of the tearing claws. After he fired, he heard the lion slide down the side of the steep roof and hit the ground with a thud in front of the door. But was he alive or dead? Uncle Dickie finally opened the door very cautiously. There, stretched out in the deep snow, was the huge lion. The carefully aimed shot had reached its mark, thus ending that particular danger to Uncle Dickie's life while serving as a snowshed inspector.

Railroad Era Activities

1. Find stories at the library about the railroader's folk heroes, Casey Jones and John Henry. Recommend some for the class to read.

2. Collect pictures to show the story of trains from the time of the first locomotive to the latest streamliners of today. Give some information about each picture.

3. Draw cartoons about some of the funny things that happened to trains in early days. (Where will you look for information to help you with these drawings?)

4. Look in music books for more folk songs about railroad workers and trains. Perhaps the class can learn some of the songs that you find.

5. Build models of famous trains. Demonstrate how they were operated. Be sure to give the history of the particular train or engine that you are demonstrating.

6. Pretend that you are a pioneer child who is going to ride on a train for the first time. You are being sent all by yourself to visit your grandparents back East. When you finally reach your grandparents' home, write back to your parents and tell them about your trip.

7. Find all the information you can as to how Indians felt about railroads crossing their land. Report this information to the class.

8. Pretend that you are a newspaper reporter for an Eastern newspaper. Describe the driving of the Golden Spike at Promontory in Utah.

CHAPTER V

SETTLING THE WEST

Life on the Sod-House Frontier

Following the Civil War, settlers flooded into Kansas and Nebraska. By 1873, they were spilling over into the Dakotas. First the prairie states, and then the plains states and mountain states, were settled. In this great region people lived farther apart than in the East, and they led much lonelier lives.

Most of these settlers claimed land under the Homestead Act, but the more prosperous paid four dollars or more an acre for railroad land. Railroads advertised their vast land holdings. They even brought in organized groups of European immigrants. Look at this photograph of one of those early newspaper advertisements. Find the cost of land. How much might it be today? What other interesting information can you find in the advertisement?

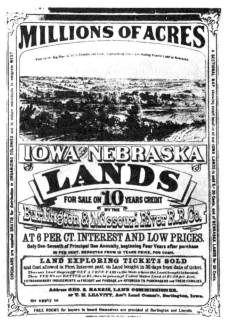

Association of American Railroads

The first thing a prairie settler did was to begin clearing the fields and plowing the land. It was important that he get his crop planted to provide food for his family.

Usually the family camped in wagons or tents until after the crops had been planted. Then, the men began the task of building some kind of shelter for their family and animals. They had no lumber since few trees grew on the prairie.

The Mandan and Pawnee Indians had solved this problem with earth lodges, so white men did the same. They cut the sod, or earth, into blocks which they laid to make walls in the way that bricks are laid. If they could find a bank of earth, they dug the back of the house into it, building only the front and part of the side walls. Poles for roof rafters were cut from the few cottonwood trees that grew along river banks. After the poles were placed on the roof, the settler spread brush, grass and more sod over them.

Sod houses weren't very nice houses. Even the floor was dirt. In this land of no-wood, canvas or leather was used to make a door. Anything but glass was used to cover a window. The "soddies" leaked when it rained. Even in dry weather, dirt, bugs and mice from the roof fell over and into everything. Sometimes even a cow wandered off a bank onto a roof and suddenly joined the family below. Women loathed the sod houses. What does this photograph tell you about life on the prairie?

The words of *Little Old Sod Shanty* described life in a sod house. The treeless prairie was the settler's new home. At times he was not happy, but he tried the best he could to make a living for himself and his family.

A Frontier Sod House

Los Angeles County Museum

Little Old Sod Shanty

Moderately fast

I am look-ing rath-er seed-y now while hold-ing down my claim,

And my vic-tuals are not al-ways served the best;

And the mice play shy-ly round me as I nes-tle down to rest,

In my lit-tle old sod shan-ty in the West.

The hin-ges are of leath-er and the win-dows have no **glass**,

While the board roof lets the howl-ing bliz-zards in,

And I hear the hun-gry coy-ote as he slinks up through the grass

Round my lit-tle old sod shan-ty on my claim.

2. Yet I rather like the novelty of living in this way,
   Though my bill of fare is always rather tame,
   But I'm happy as a clam on the land of Uncle Sam
   In the little old sod shanty on my claim.
   But when I left my Eastern home, a bachelor so gay,
   To try and win my way to wealth and fame,
   I little thought I'd come down to burning twisted hay
   In the little old sod shanty on my claim.

3. My clothes are plastered o'er with dough, I'm looking like a fright,
   And everything is scattered round the room,
   But I wouldn't give the freedom that I have out in the West
   For the table of the Eastern man's old home.
   Still I wish that some kindhearted girl would pity on me take,
   And relieve me from the mess that I am in;
   The angel how I'd bless her if this her home she'd make
   In the little old sod shanty on my claim.

4. And we would make our fortune on the prairies of the West,
   Just as happy as two lovers we'd remain;
   We'd forget the trials and troubles we endured at the first,
   In the little old sod shanty on my claim.
   And if fate should bless us with now and then an heir,
   To cheer our hearts with honest pride of fame,
   Oh, then we'd be contented for the toil that we had spent
   In the little old sod shanty on our claim.

"Little Old Sod Shanty" from *The American Songbag* by Carl Sandburg. Published by Harcourt, Brace and World, Inc.

Most of the people who lived on the sod-house frontier were very poor. About their only pleasure was in visiting each other. A lonely settler, looking out the window on Sunday morning, might see a neighbor coming across the prairie in his big wagon. Soon the visiting family arrived and came in to spend the day. Their clothes might be ragged, but people knew that others were poor, too, so there was no embarrasment.

Carl Sandburg described the song, *Dakota Land*, as a psalm of a desolate people. When you read the words to this song you will understand what he meant.

Dakota Land

1. We've reached the land of des - ert sweet, Where noth - ing grows for man to eat, The wind it blows with fev - 'rish heat A - cross the plains so hard to beat.

Chorus

O Da - ko - ta land, sweet Da - ko - ta land As on thy fier - y soil I stand, I look a - cross the plains, And won - der why it nev - er rains, Till Ga - briel blows his trum - pet sound, And says the rain's just gone a - round.

2. We've reached the land of hills and stones
   Where all is strewn with buffalo bones.
   O buffalo bones, bleached buffalo bones,
   I seem to hear your sighs and moans.

3. We have no wheat, we have no oats,
   We have no corn to feed our shoats;
   Our chickens are so very poor
   They beg for crumbs outside the door.

4. Our horses are of bronco race;
   Starvation stares them in the face.
   We do not live, we only stay;
   We are too poor to get away.

"Dakota Land" from *The American Songbag* by Carl Sandburg. Used by permission of Harcourt, Brace and World, Inc.

Pioneers Helped Each Other

One of the first types of social activity in a new prairie community was the "bee." For a "house-raising bee" to help a new settler, neighbors came from near and far. The day's work closed with a feast which the neighborhood women prepared while the men "raised" the house.

A family's misfortune was also the occasion for a bee. Word went around and neighbors assembled to help. It might be to husk corn, plow, haul wood or plant crops. No one thought of pay. On occasion a public project such as building a schoolhouse, a church or a bridge brought neighbors together in good fellowship.

Dances and Play-Parties

Of all frontier amusements, dancing probably held first place in popularity. Every new building that went up in the prairie towns was an excuse for holding a "house-warming" dance. Among church people who objected to dancing, the house-warming custom was varied. Instead of dancing they enjoyed a good meal and play-party songs or singing games. At this kind of party, young people went through certain steps similar to those of dancing but without instrumental music. Instead of playing musical instruments, they sang songs. See if you can make up a dance to this play-party song.

Skip to My Lou

1. Fly in the but-ter-milk, shoo, fly, shoo!
Fly in the but-ter-milk, shoo, fly, shoo!
Fly in the but-ter-milk, shoo, fly, shoo!
Skip to my lou, my dar - ling.
Lou, lou, skip to my lou, Lou, lou, skip to my lou!
Lou, lou, skip to my lou, Skip to my lou, my dar - ling.

2. Going to Texas, two by two.
3. Lost my partner, what'll I do?
4. I'll get another, prettier than you.
5. Can't get a red bird, a blue bird'll do.
6. Chickens in the haystack, two by two.
7. Pig's in the fence, and can't get through.
8. Hurry up, slow poke, do and do.
9. Skip a little faster, this'll never do.
10. Little red wagon, painted blue.
11. Back from Texas, how do you do?

Games for All Ages

At other parties such games as "Ring-Around-the-Rosy," "Drop the Handkerchief," "Paying Forfeits" and "Old Mother Wobble Gobble" were popular.

In the Old Mother Wobble Gobble game, the players were seated in a circle around a leader. The leader began by reciting: "Old Mother Wobble Gobble, pray pity you; Old Mother Wobble Gobble, do as I do." Then the leader would do some ridiculous thing. The rest of the group were to imitate him. Those who were unable to imitate the leader forfeited some personal belonging such as a ring, handkerchief or necktie. Forfeits were redeemed in the following manner. Someone held the object to be redeemed over the head of the one who decided what had to be done to get the forefeit back, saying, "Heavy, heavy hangs over thy head; what shall the owner do to redeem it?" The person in the circle over whose head the object was held asked, "Fine or superfine?" The person holding the object answered, "Fine," if it belonged to a man, or "Superfine," if it belonged to a woman. Then the penalty was given. One popular penalty was, "Pick three cherries with Julie." Whereupon Julie would come forward blushing and the gentleman would kiss her three times.

Winter Activities

The lyceum, or literary society, was a regular winter activity. The programs listed recitations, songs, dialogues, debates, essays and tableaux. So popular were literary societies that lyceums were held in frontier towns under the open sky before there were country schoolhouses or other buildings for meeting places. Anyone who wanted to perform was listed on the program. It was popular to memorize and recite poems. This was the kind of poem that might have been recited. It was written by John Greenleaf Whittier. You might like to find other poems written by him that tell about the early settlement of our county.

We cross the prairies as of old
   The pilgrims crossed the sea,
To make the West, as they the East,
   The homestead of the free!

We go to rear a wall of men
   On Freedom's southern line,
And plant beside the cotton-tree
   The rugged Northern pine!
             —Whittier

"The Kansas Emigrants" (July, 1854) by John Greenleaf Whittier.

Reading matter was very scarce and anything readable was popular with the more intellectual people. Almanacs and patent medicine pamphlets were issued by the medicine companies and given away at the stores. Much of the reading matter in these pamphlets consisted of proverbs and sayings, many of them taken from *Poor Richard's Almanac.*

Spell-Downs

In the 1860's and 1870's, spelling schools were popular. Young and old people attended these gatherings which were held every week or so at the schoolhouse during the winter months. Sides were chosen and some competent person, usually the schoolteacher, was selected to "give out" the words.

Two system were used. In "chase the fox," the team spelling the most words correctly was named the winner. In the other system, the "spell-down," the pronouncer alternated between two lines of standing spellers. When a contestant missed a word, he sat down. The person who stood the longest had spelled down the crowd and won the contest for his side.

Ciphering Contests

With the introduction of blackboards in the late 1870's "ciphering" matches became a popular amusement. Each neighborhood had its champions whom they would match against all newcomers. As more and more skill was displayed, addition and simple problems gave way to square and cube roots.

Activities for Young Grown-Ups

Before settlers could afford buggies, young couples went horseback riding on the prairie. Ordinarily, each person had his own horse. The young ladies rode side-saddle and dressed in riding skirts that had buckshot in the hem to hold them down and insure modesty.

"Joy riding" in a lumber wagon drawn by oxen or horses was a common type of amusement. Often on a winter Sunday afternoon, well-bundled-up groups would partially fill the wagon with hay and take joy rides through the nearby countryside.

Hayride

Young people on a hayride might have sung a song much like this one:

Hayride

Music and Words by Richard C. Berg

Rhythmically

Come on a - long, we're go - ing for a hay - ride,

Fill up the wag - on with a load of hay;

Come on a - long, we're go - ing for a hay - ride,

Frost's on the pump - kin, au - tumn's on its way.

Gid - dy up, Dob - bin, oh, here we go a - jog - ging

O - ver the hills and far a - way.

Come on a - long, we're go - ing for a hay - ride;

Sing and be mer - ry, have a hap - py day.

"Hayride" from *Studying Music, Music for Young Americans, Second Edition*, Book 4, by Richard C. Berg, Lee Kjelson, Eugene W. Troth, Daniel S. Hooley, and Josephine Wolverton. American Book Company, copyright 1966.

Other Kinds of Parties

Surprise parties were quite the fashion in the "good old days." Often a load of merry-makers made their way across the prairie to some lonely cabin. The "Whoa, haw, gee!" of the driver was the signal that aroused the early-retiring family.

"Taffy pulls" were held in the winter in homes or at the country schoolhouse. People of all ages attended. Young men and their partners had fun pulling the long ropes of candy. If it was too soft, it stuck to your hands and you had to eat it off! If there were some left, you could take it home.

Certain special days were celebrated with great enthusiasm. Fourth of July, Washington's Birthday, and Valentine's Day were all festive occasions. Thanksgiving was more of a religious event. A church service was held in the morning, after which a great feast was served. Wild game, hunted nearby, provided meat for the community dinner.

There was little opportunity to have an evergreen Christmas tree since none grew on the prairie. Usually another kind of tree was decorated with strings of popcorn and other homemade ornaments. There were few presents, but a program was almost always presented at the community Christmas party at the schoolhouse.

Manners and Customs

People were hospitable and neighborly on the sod-house frontier. As the settlers battled against Indians, heat, drought, insects, wind, tornadoes and loneliness, they were drawn together. A man might ride across the prairie for days, hunting for stray cattle or horses. He was welcome to stay at different settlers' homes, and was never asked to pay for his board and lodging or for his horse's food. If a man wanted to pay, the reply would always be, "That's all right, neighbor. You'd do the same for me if I came your way."

When a stranger happened in at meal-time, there was always an invitation from the head of the house to bring up a chair. If a woman headed the household she said, "Now, you just make yourself perfectly at home, and help yourself to anything you see!"

As a rule, neighbors were willing to share anything they owned. No man driving along with an empty wagon would pass another without inviting him to ride. If he had a loaded wagon and happened to overtake a woman walking, he would ask her to ride even if it meant that he would have to walk.

It was not considered good taste for a stranger to walk directly up to a settler's home and knock on the door. Instead, it was polite to first shout a greeting while still in his wagon or on his horse. The greeting was usually, "Hello!" or "Hello, the house!"

If, after watching the stranger through their windows, the settlers decided he was friendly and acceptable, they would open the door and say, "Come in, stranger!" After this, it was all right for the stranger to get down and accept their invitation.

The song, *Wayfaring Stranger*, expresses some of the feelings that lonely, religious people might have had as they traveled through strange frontiers, far from their loved ones. Turn the page to read the words of this song.

Wayfaring Stranger

I'm just a poor way-far-ing stran - ger

A - trav - 'ling through this world of woe;

But there's no sick - ness, toil nor dan - ger

In that bright world to which I go.

I'm go - ing there to see my { fa - ther, moth - er, sis - ter, broth - er, }

I'm go - ing there no more to roam,

I'm just a - go - ing o - ver Jor - dan,

I'm just a - go - ing o - ver home.

Home of Early Settlers — Montana

CHAPTER VI

LIFE ON THE ALASKAN FRONTIER

There was a gold rush in the Alaskan Klondike in 1897 and 1898. After the gold rush was over, a few of the prospectors stayed in Alaska. They were called "sourdoughs"—a strange name that came from a kind of wilderness yeast that was used in making bread. The prospectors usually kept some of this yeast in a pot. By adding a little flour and water occasionally, the yeast lasted for many years. When some of the yeast was mixed with batter, it produced delicious sourdough flapjacks and biscuits.

Some of the sourdough prospectors continued to search for gold while others turned to hunting and trapping. The latter discovered that this new frontier was filled with surprises. There were great herds of caribou, huge valleys with fine farming and grazing lands, and almost unlimited resources in fish and furs.

Sourdough Prospectors   *Los Angeles County Museum*

Native Folklore of Alaska

Settlers in Alaska learned that the native Indians and Eskimos are rich in their folklore. Although some of their songs, dances, and folk tales seem unique, there is a certain similarity to those of other primitive people of North America.

Eskimo Folk Tales

Until recent years, Eskimos looked for leadership to "witch-doctors" who were believed to have supernatural powers. Each witch doctor was said to have a special "control" that would do his bidding. However, according to legend, the witch-doctors on Seward Peninsula were ruined when the first white man came.

The white man with his native guide stopped one evening to camp in a deserted Eskimo house. The guide told the white man that they should go on, because the devil often stopped to rest in this particular place. The white man ignored the warning. That night, as they sat eating, in came the devil. The poor Eskimo trembled with fear and covered himself with bedding. The devil and the white man had a terrible battle. The white man won and the devil took to his heels, leaving the country completely.

It is said that all witch-doctors lost their powers at that moment. But the tales of their many activities form the basis for almost all Eskimo folk stories. These stories are usually chanted. Most of them have a definite moral, but some are merely funny. Read this tale about an Eskimo boy who ate too much. What lesson do you think it teaches?

The Boy Who Ate Too Much

A small boy once lived in an Eskimo house with an old, old woman. This boy was always hungry and he was always begging for food. One day, when the last of the food was eaten, the old woman sent him down to the beach to search for more.

The first thing he found was a little tomcod. He picked it up and, after pulling off its head, swallowed it at one gulp. Continuing his search, he presently came upon a seal. As before, he pulled off its head and ate the whole seal. On he went, still hungry, until he came upon a large bearded seal, or oogrook, sunning itself on the sand. Before the oogrook could slide back into the water, the boy had caught it, pulled off its head and eaten it. Still not satisfied, he continued down the beach until he caught sight of a white whale stranded high and dry on the sand. In the same manner as he had done with the tomcod, the seal, and the oogrook, he pulled off its head and ate the whale—skin, bone, blubber and all.

After the boy had finished the whale he felt better. Presently he began to sing. He rubbed his belly and sang to his stomach. For the first time in his life he had had enough to eat. But soon he became very, very thirsty, so he went to a nearby pond and drank until the pond was quite dry. Then he started off for the house in which he lived with the old woman.

"The Boy Who Ate Too Much" from *Igloo Tales* by Edward L. Keithahn. Used by permission of the author.

Reaching the house, he tried to get in the door but he could not get through. He had eaten too much.

"How am I to get in?" he called to the old woman.

"Come through the window," she answered.

The window was much smaller than the door, but he tried it anyway and found he could just get his head through.

"I can't get through the window," he called to the old woman.

"Come in through the ventilator," she cried in answer.

This seemed ridiculous to the boy since the ventilator was very much smaller than the window, but he tried it anyway. This time he got his head and shoulders through but he could go no further. Again he called to the old woman for advice.

"Come through the eye of my needle," she shouted.

She held up the needle and through it the boy came tumbling onto the floor.

When the old woman saw how swelled he was from eating so much, she shouted, "Look out! Keep away from the seal oil lamp!"

But in spite of himself the boy stumbled towards the lamp. The old woman barely had time to rush out the door. Boom! There was a mighty explosion. When the old woman crawled up to the window and peered in, the boy and the lamp had disappeared. But in the room there was a deep, dark pool, and in it were swimming a tomcod, a seal, an oogrook, and a big white whale.

Legends of the Totem Pole

In the beautiful timber land of Southeastern Alaska, where many of the Alaskan Indians live, is an area of interesting totem poles made by early tribes. It is said by some people that the strange, interlocked figures on a totem pole reveal their meaning only to certain of the tribesmen and never to outsiders.

Actually there is nothing "hidden" in totem poles that cannot be revealed with patience and study. This, of course, applies only to totem poles containing a story, for not all types are meant to tell a story.

The mortuary pole consisted of a plain pole on top of which was a box containing ashes of the dead. Later, a totem figure was placed at the top and the ashes moved to a place in back of the pole. This type of totem pole, the most common one found in Alaska, was replaced in later times by Christian burial.

The family pole was a type placed against the middle front of the house with a hole near its base to be used as a doorway to the house. It was beautifully carved and painted. Its legend was from the mythological history of the family living within the house.

Another type of totem is called the "ridicule," or "shame" pole. It was generally erected to shame or to make fun of some person of high standing for failing to take care of his duties or obligations.

Memorial poles were erected much in the same manner as tomb stones, although at a distance from the grave. They were not raised for the dead alone; they could also honor the living.

Family Pole or House Pillar

House pillars supported the central rafters of the community house of certain tribes. Usually four of these pillars were used. Their carvings illustrated myths from that tribe's history. Because these pillars were indoors and not exposed to the weather, many of them are very old and well-preserved.

The most recent type of totem is the "Potlatch Pole." Newly-rich tribal chiefs tried to out-do each other by erecting elaborately carved poles, sixty to eighty feet tall.

Find out more about the totem poles of Alaska.

Memorial Pole

Ridicule Pole

Mortuary Pole

One of the adventures of Kayak, a mythological Tlingit hero, is described in this legend:

The One-Legged
Fisherman Totem Pole

Kayak's father, Lakishina, was a wolfish man who delighted in killing his children by sawing them to death on the spines of his red cod-skin coat. For some years, Kayak's mother had saved him and a brother and sister by changing them into puppies whenever their father was home.

Kayak finally grew strong enough to kill his father. However, by a strange curse, Kayak's sister was forbidden ever to look upon her brothers, on pain that if she did, they would be turned to stone.

One day Kayak and his brother, learning that there was a fisherman at Yakutat who had a magic harpoon, journeyed there in hopes of obtaining it. The fisherman turned out to be a supernatural creature, something like an eagle, except that he had only one leg. By means of the magic harpoon he secured salmon easily, strung them on ropes, and then flew to his home in a grizzly-bear's den far up the creek.

The coat worn by the fisherman was ornamented with two bear's heads. When the fisherman arrived home, the bear's heads removed the salmon from the strings. One head tossed fish to a large male grizzly, and the other tossed fish to an old female bear who was the mother-in-law of the fisherman since he was married to her daughter.

On the following day Kayak, who

had observed all this, dressed in the skin of a sea monster he had killed in an earlier adventure at Sitka. Then Kayak hid underwater at the place where the salmon were schooled together. When the fisherman came down and threw his magic harpoon at a salmon, Kayak grasped it. Cutting the

"The One-Legged Fisherman Totem Pole" from *Monuments in Cedar* by Edward L. Keithahn. Published by Superior Publishing Company, Seattle, Washington. Used by permission.

line, he swam under-water with the coveted weapon until he could emerge unseen.

But sometime later the fisherman caught Kayak with the harpoon in his hand. In their struggle, Kayak killed the fisherman. Kayak then skinned him and got into his hide with the intention of deceiving the fisherman's wife. She, however, was not fooled and, together with her grizzly bear parents, attacked Kayak. In the battle which followed, all the bears were killed, and Kayak went on to more adventures.

At last Kayak and his brother met their end crossing the Stikine River. The current was swift, and their sister, fearing they might be swept away, looked up at them, whereupon both were instantly turned to solid stone. The stones are still pointed out to travelers on the Stikine River not very far from Wrangell.

Eskimo Dance-Songs

Most Eskimo songs are dance-songs. These songs are not sung out-doors, for Eskimos believe that a spirit, carrying away their words, might rob them of the breath of life. So Eskimos sing in a dance house, which is really the social center of their community. Men, women and children gather there during stormy days and on winter evenings to sing and dance. They like to entertain visitors from other communities. Almost every Eskimo can sing and dance with as much skill as he can hunt. The person who can compose a song for a special occasion is important to his community, so almost everyone tries to make up songs.

Here is an Alaskan folk song that was created by a Coppermine River native. Like most primitive songs, it deals with things that concern the singer in his daily life—in this case, hunting and fishing.

Eskimo Land

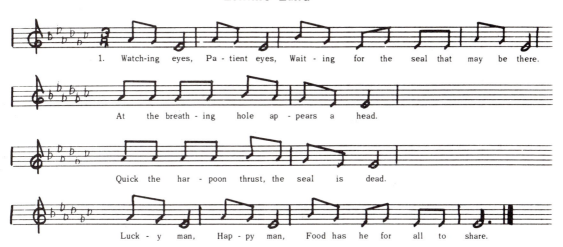

1. Watch-ing eyes, Pa - tient eyes, Wait - ing for the seal that may be there.

At the breath - ing hole ap - pears a head.

Quick the har - poon thrust, the seal is dead.

Luck - y man, Hap - py man, Food has he for all to share.

2. Busy days,
   Fishing days,
   Upstream run of salmon has begun.
   Traps of stone their journey will delay.
   Thrusting harpoons find them easy prey.
   Thankful days,
   Feasting days,
   Food for winter has been won.

3. Stamping feet,
   Testing feet,
   For an igloo, firm the snow must be.
   Sharp the knife that cuts the blocks of snow.
   Strong the hand that sets them row on row.
   Now for rest,
   Sheltered rest,
   Though the winds blow from the sea.

"Eskimo Land" from *Music Near and Far,* copyright 1956, 1962, Silver Burdett Company. Used by permission.

Eskimo Dances

In an Eskimo dance, everyone first stands facing the drummer. The drummer holds a drum made from a circular whale bone covered with moose or caribou hide. As he begins to chant, the drummer keeps the rhythm by striking the underside of the whale bone with a kind of baton. Then men, women and children all move into a circle to interpret the chant with arm and body motions. Their dance step is a kind of shuffle.

Eskimo Arts and Crafts

The Eskimo people have a strong sense of beauty. Although they have little time for art in itself, they like to decorate the objects they use everyday. They are skilled in working with wood and they carve beautiful objects out of bone and ivory. They might make the buckles for kayak thongs in the shapes of seals, or they might carve a knife handle in the shape of a fish or a man. Almost everything they make, from the smallest needed object to the largest boat, shows their sense of artistic form and their love of good design and fine craftsmanship.

Alaskan Frontier Days Activities

1. Find more Eskimo folk tales and dance-songs in books at the library. Report to the class about them.
2. Select "The Natural Resources of Alaska" as a research topic. Report the information you find to the class in a written form. Include pictures and drawings.
3. Design some totem poles. Have them tell a story. (Where will you look for information about how to do this?)
4. Try to get some "wilderness yeast." Keep it in a pot and observe what happens. Perhaps you can make some sourdough pancakes.
5. Look in library books for Alaskan Indian legends. Share these with the class.
6. Explain the meaning of "Seward's Folly." Find some of the cartoons that were drawn about this topic.
7. Try writing a poem or a folk tale about an Eskimo boy and his adventures while hunting.
8. Find out more about the gold rush to Alaska. Explain why families did not go along.

CHAPTER VII

TYING A NATION TOGETHER

Before railroads were built there had been great interest in road building. When railroads did come, people thought they were the final answer to man's transportation needs. They began to say that roads were no longer needed because steel rails could carry more people and freight both farther and faster. Most roads were very seldom repaired, so they began to break up.

Compare these two pictures of "wheel-men." What can you say about the two types of bicycles? What information can you get about roads from the picture?

Wheelmen were the first to come to the rescue of the neglected roads. Wheelmen were not automobilists, as you might suppose. They were outdoor men and women who rode the new "safety" bicyles. They campaigned actively for better roads.

Library of Congress

Bureau of Public Roads

The national bicycle craze started in Boston in 1877. By 1900 there were about thirty million bicycles of all kinds in the United States. Without good roads, bicycle riding was limited. The bicyclists organized into local and national clubs. They called themselves the "League of American Wheelmen." They kept on asking that local and national governments do something about improving the roads.

By 1900 a more important force joined the drive for better roads. With the success of the gasoline engine came production of the "horseless carriage" by R. E. Olds, Henry Ford and others.

The horseless carriage, or automobile, as it soon came to be called, couldn't travel over bad roads as the horse and buggy could. This led to much teasing and joking by people who were still traveling in the old way. As they happened upon a "gasoline buggy" stuck in the mud or having engine trouble, they might call out, "Get a horse!"

During this difficult period for automobile owners, it was not unusual to have to pay a farmer to bring his team of horses to pull one's automobile out of the mud.

How would you interpret this picture?

Stuck in the Mud

By 1916, roads were improved in some places, and the transcontinental Lincoln Highway was under construction. But people who crossed country or state lines were apt to plunge from a good road into a mud hole. What would you do if you were the driver of the first car in this picture?

During the early days of the automobile, many people were anxious to get into the business of building them. Before 1900 there were some 300 makes of automobiles. Bicycle repair shops became automobile factories. Many songs were written about the new "contraption." Tales were told about the advantages of this way of traveling. One folk tale was about a man named Hank Lord who wanted *everything* on wheels.

Hank, the Free Wheeler

When Hank Lord was still in diapers, he cried until his poor old Dad had to rollerskate the floor with him instead of walking to and fro like it was proper for fathers to do.

He pulled his lunch to the little red schoolhouse in a little red wagon. He even tried to make the cows learn to ride bicycles so they would make better time coming from the pasture when he called them for milking. He traveled around the barnyard so fast that, long before anybody ever heard of an automobile, Hank had to wear goggles to keep the bugs out of his eyes. In fact, he was called "Speedrow" in five states and twenty counties when the Indianapolis racing track was still a hayfield, a frog-puddle, and a couple of turnip patches. Hank was speed on wheels; he knew good and well that wheels made the world go round.

"Hank, the Free Wheeler" adapted from *A Treasury of American Folklore*, edited by B. A. Botkin. New York: Crown Publishers, Inc.

When he started his automobile factory, a man could have walked from front to back and from ceiling to floor without seeing more than a few trucks and wheelbarrows and such. In those days in an automobile factory, a bunch of men got around in a ring. Pretty soon here came one man with a part of an automobile frame. He laid it down on the floor. Then he was followed by other men who kept bringing pieces until finally there were enough to start working on. Then all the men in the ring started reaming, banging, boring and bolting until it looked as if they had a "thing" that might take a snifter of gasoline and go skedaddling down the road to a fare-thee-well.

Hank decided that iron cost too much and lasted too long to use in making his automobiles, so he got to looking around the back alleys for every tin can he could lay his hands on. He made "tin flivvers" out of them. As long as they held together long enough to get outside the factory gates, he never worried his mind about them. He just hollered: "More tin! More wheels! Roll 'em, boys' roll 'em!"

It got so people couldn't throw a pork-and-beans can in the alley that it wasn't picked up and hustled right along to Hank's factory. The little children on street corners and in vacant lots began to sing:

"There was an old man, he had a wooden leg,

He had no auto nor no auto could he beg.

He got two spools and an old tin can;

He made him a flivver and the darned thing ran!"

Hank's factory ran at full speed. He put his automobiles together faster and faster.

But a man's got wheels, same as a factory. No matter how much oil is poured on them, they finally wear out. And so Hank's bearings began to fall apart and there wasn't a thing to be done. Old age took its toll.

They sent his coffin down the assembly line nice and slow, out of respect for the dead. Then six pallbearers picked it up to carry it to the hearse. They almost dropped the coffin when Hank reared up and smashed the glass and yelled:

"What is this? You call this efficiency? Put this thing on wheels!"

A Plane at Kitty Hawk

In 1903, a Winton was the first automobile to cross the continent from San Francisco to New York. Less than five months later on the sandy beach of Kitty Hawk, North Carolina, Orville Wright made man's first successful flight through the air. In 1911, the first transcontinental flight was made from New York to California.

Together, the automobile and the airplane transformed America. Together they fulfilled, as the Pony Express riders had failed to do, the dream of bringing the great West into a closer union with the rest of the nation.

Our Pioneers Are Honored

When the 1850's arrived, the United States stretched from coast to coast and our flag flew over an area of 3,000,000 square miles. Pioneers had gone from the East and the Mississippi Valley into Texas, Utah, California, and the Oregon country. Pioneers from Illinois had started the settlements that grew into the great city of Seattle, Washington.

Throughout our country there are monuments to honor these brave people. On one that stands on the shores of Puget Sound in the state of Washington is a poem that conveys thoughts for all Americans to remember and cherish.

Who do you think were the pioneers?
Grizzled old men with rifles? and wives
With wrinkled faces that showed their fears
And the worries they had all their lives?

Twenty-four people stood in the rain
On the shore of Elliott Bay,
All had come over mountain and plain
Except Rolland and Livvy, born on the way.

Lenora, John and Virginia were four,
Minerva was two that fall,
Olive was five when she stood on that shore,
Alonzo was seven, but tall.

Louisa, they said, was little for seven,
Mary and Laura had lived nine years,
Gertrude had only just passed eleven—
Who do you think were the pioneers?

—Author Unknown

As you come to the close of this book, keep thinking about your American ancestors. Find out about things that happened to them. Lock the stories in your heart and remember to tell them with pride to your children and grandchildren. They, in turn, will carry the stories on to other generations. In this way, pride in our great American heritage will never be lost even as we continue to explore our latest frontier—outer space.

This Land Is Your Land

Words and Music by Woody Guthrie

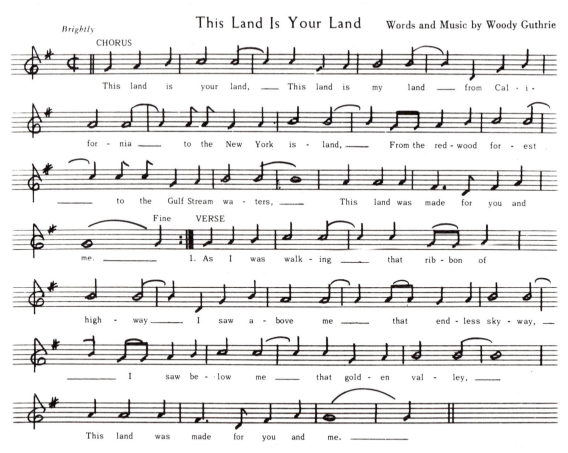

Brightly

CHORUS

This land is your land, __ This land is my land __ from Cal-i-for-nia __ to the New York is-land, __ From the red-wood for-est __ to the Gulf Stream wa-ters, __ This land was made for you and me. __

Fine VERSE

1. As I was walk-ing __ that rib-bon of high-way __ I saw a-bove me __ that end-less sky-way, __ I saw be-low me __ that gold-en val-ley, __ This land was made for you and me. __

VERSE 2. I've roamed and rambled, and I followed my footsteps
To the sparkling sands of her diamond deserts,
And all around me, a voice was sounding,
This land was made for you and me.

"This Land Is Your Land" from *22 Favorite Folk Songs*, published by The Richmond Organization, New York.

Bicycle and Horseless Carriage Days Activities

1. Make a collection of pictures of early automobile models. Give the history of each automobile. Display these pictures for the class.

2. Find information about the first men who manufactured automobiles. Describe how their factories compared with the factories of today.

3. Make a scrapbook of songs, stories and pictures about "horseless carriage" days. Perhaps the class can learn some of the songs.

4. Invite an antique car club member to talk to your class. Perhaps he can arrange for you to take a ride in one of his cars.

5. Collect or draw pictures of bicycles that show the development from the first high-wheelers to the modern racing bicycles.

6. Write a story about this situation: A "buggy" horse, that always had been the pride and joy of a particular family, was suddenly turned out to pasture when the family bought one of the "new-fangled, horseless carriages." The horse now had nothing to do except stand by the fence and watch the family drive away in their new vehicle. He no longer felt wanted or useful.

Airplanes and Space Ships Activities

1. Do a research project on the Wright brothers. Find all the information you can about them and report this in written form for your class.

2. Find songs and poems that were written about early airplanes. Make a scrapbook of this collection. Your class might like to learn some of the songs.

3. Collect or draw pictures that show the development of the airplane from Kitty Hawk to the latest jet and rocket. Give information about each airplane.

4. Start a scrapbook on space travel. Plan for pages to be added as our country's space exploration continues. Include newspaper and magazine articles and pictures. Now imagine that you are suddenly projected fifty years into the future. You are showing this scrapbook to your great-grandchildren. Write a story that describes this experience.

5. Make models of different types of planes and give information about each kind.

A

adobe — a brick or building material of sun-dried earth and straw.

Allegheny Mountains — part of the Appalachian mountain range of the eastern United States, extending from central Pennsylvania southward through western Maryland, eastern West Virginia, and western Virginia.

almanac — a publication containing astronomical and meteorological data by the days, weeks, and months of a year and often containing other information.

ancestors — one from whom a person is descended and who is usually more remote in the line of descent than a grandparent.

antediluvian — 1. of or relating to the period before the flood described in the Bible; 2. made, evolved, or developed a long time ago; antiquated.

Appalachian Mountains — the oldest mountains in the United States, stretching from Quebec in Canada to central Alabama.

apprehensive — uneasy or fearful about something that may happen; quick to learn or to understand.

aristocrat — one who has the manners and viewpoint typical of the aristocracy or upper class.

assembly line — an arrangement of machines, equipment and workers in which work passes from task to task in direct line until the product is assembled.

attire — the clothing or dress.

axeman — one who fells trees and chops or splits logs with a tool having a heavy-edged head fixed to a handle and the edge parallel to the handle.

B

bandana — a large figured handkerchief or kerchief, usually red or blue with a white pattern.

bandolies — small musical instruments resembling a lute.

Beatitudes — the verses in the Sermon on the Mount, all of which begin with "Blessed," as "Blessed are the poor in spirit." Matthew 5:3-12.

blacksmith — one who forges or shapes iron while it is hot.

braggart — a loud, arrogant boaster.

brambles — rough, prickly shrubs or vines.

brigade — a group of people organized for a special activity.

boat lamp — a boat-shaped shallow dish filled with grease which burned by means of a wick.

bodacious — dialect, meaning impudent, impertinent, saucy, forward, smarty, discourteous.

bayous — arms or outlets of lakes or rivers, usually marshy or sluggish bodies of water.

box canyon — a canyon with steep, high walls on three sides.

C

calico-printed cotton cloth — a plain white cotton fabric with figured patterns.

calliope — a musical instrument with a series of whistles played by keys arranged as in an organ.

carded the wool — cleansed, disentangled and collected together the fibers of the wool by use of a card before the spinning.

caribou — any of several large palmate-antlered deer of northern North America that are related to the reindeer.

castoffs — articles thrown away or aside; abandoned.

ceded or signed-over — yielded or granted (typically) by treaty.

chantey — a song sung by sailors in rhythm to their work.

chanteymen — sailors who head the singing in rhythm to their work.

Chicago Road — a pioneer road across the state of Michigan.

Chickasaw Indians — an Indian people originally in northern Mississippi and Alabama.

Chickasaw Trace — a trail or route that was first used by the Chickasaw Indians in attacks on neighboring tribes in northern Mississippi, western Tennessee, and northern Alabama.

chipping the bark of "witness trees" — mark made on a tree by chipping off a piece of the bark.

Choctaw Indians — an Indian people originally in Mississippi, Alabama, and Louisiana.

cholera — any of several diseases of man usually marked by severe gastrointestinal symptoms.

cider — the juice of apples used as a drink and for making vinegar or other products.

ciphering — to use figures in a mathematical process.

circuit — an accustomed tour, as by a traveling judge or preacher, around an assigned district or territory.

cloth fulling parties — parties at which people sat in a circle and stamped their bare feet on woolen cloth that had been placed on the floor and wet with warm water.

cobbler — a mender or maker of shoes and often of other leather goods.

Comanche Indians — an Indian people originally ranging from Wyoming and Nebraska south into New Mexico and northwestern Texas.

contraption — contrivance, gadget.

cooper or barrel-maker — one who makes or repairs wooden barrels or tubs.

crackers — something that makes a snapping or cracking noise.

cricket — term applied to certain grasshoppers or locusts.

croup — a spasmodic laryngitis, especially of young children, marked by attacks of difficult breathing and a hoarse metallic cough.

Cumberland Gap — a natural pass through the Appalachian Mountains, at the meeting point of Virginia, Kentucky, and Tennessee, used as a gateway to the West by pioneer settlers.

Cumberland Mountains — a part of the Appalachian Mountain system, extending across part of eastern Tennessee and Kentucky and forming the boundary between Virginia and Kentucky.

D

debate — to discuss a question by considering opposed arguments.

dialogue — a conversation between two or more persons.

diesel — a vehicle driven by a diesel engine.

diligently — steady, earnest, and energetic application and effort.

disintegrate — to break into parts.

diversion — something that diverts or amuses; a pastime.

drought — a prolonged period of dryness.

E

emigrants — people who leave a place of abode or a country for life or residence elsewhere.

ensue — to take place afterward or as a result.

Erie Canal — the first important national waterway built in the United States. Crossing New York from Buffalo on Lake Erie to Troy and Albany on the Hudson River, it was completed in 1825.

escapade — an adventurous action that runs counter to approval or ordinary conduct.

essay — an analytic or interpretive literary composition usually dealing with its subject from a personal point of view.

expedite — to send out promptly.

F

fiddle — a violin.

flash flood — a very sudden, violent flooding of a river or stream.

flax — a slender annual plant with blue flowers commonly grown for its fiber and seed.

flickers or movies — pertaining to the first moving pictures.

flintlock rifle — a rifle having a flint in the hammer for striking a spark to ignite the charge.

foliage — the mass of leaves of a plant.

forfeit — to lose the right to something by some error.

fulling or pre-shrinking — to shrink and thicken woolen cloth by moistening, heating, and pressing.

G

gentility — courtesy.

geometric pattern — a pattern or design consisting of straight lines, circles, triangles, etc.

glutton — one that eats too much.

goad — a pointed rod used to urge on an animal.

grasshopper, also called locust — any of numerous leaping insects having migratory habits, often traveling in vast swarms destroying crops and vegetation.

grist mill — a mill for grinding a batch of grain, the product including the flour or meal and the grain offals.

groom or horse-tender — a man or boy in charge of horses.

gunsmith — a person who makes guns.

H

half-comic superhero — a legendary somewhat amusing figure often of divine descent endowed with unusually great strength and ability.

hanks — a coiled or looped bundle of wool yarn.

harpoon — a barbed spear used especially in hunting large fish or whales.

Hartford — presently the capital and largest city of Connecticut, established as a trading post by the Dutch in 1623.

hetchels — pieces of wood through which iron spikes had been driven—used for straightening or combing the fibers of wool.

Homestead Act — legislative act of law authorizing the sale of public lands in homesteads to settlers.

horse trough — a long, shallow, often V-shaped receptacle for the drinking water or feed of horses.

hospitable — given to generous and cordial reception of guests.

hostile — unfriendly.

I

infare — a reception for a newly married couple.

inn — a public house for the lodging and entertainment of travelers.

intellectual — given to study, reflection, and speculation.

Isthmus of Panama — the narrow strip of land which connects North and South America.

J

jackal — any of several Old World wild dogs smaller than the related wolves.

jehus — drivers of coaches or cabs.

jester — one given to making witty or funny remarks.

Jew's harp — a small lyre-shaped instrument that when placed between the teeth gives tones from a metal tongue struck by the finger.

K

kayak — an Eskimo canoe made of skins stretched over a light frame of wood or bone with an opening in the middle for a person.

L

lamp black — a fine, bulky, dull-black soot deposited in the incomplete burning of lamp oil.

last or model — a wooden or metal form which is shaped like the human foot and over which a shoe is repaired or shaped.

leach — to dissolve out alkali by the action of water poured through ashes.

linsey-woolsey cloth — a coarse sturdy fabric of wool and linen or cotton.

loom — a frame or machine for interlacing at right angles two or more sets of threads or yarns to form a cloth.

Louisiana Purchase — the purchase of Louisiana and the rest of the Mississippi Valley region from France by the United States in 1803 for the sum of $15,000,000.

Louisiana Territory — the huge territory of Louisiana and the Mississippi region which was purchased by the United States from France in 1803.

lyceum or literary society — an association providing public lectures, concerts, and entertainment.

lye — a strong alkaline liquid rich in potassium carbonate leached from wood ashes and used especially in soap-making and washing.

M

masquerade — an action or appearance that is a mere disguise or outward show.

metamorphosed — transformed or changed.

militia — the whole body of able-bodied male citizens declared by law as being subject to call to military service.

moral — expressing or teaching a lesson of right behavior.

mythological history — history of the myths dealing with the gods, demigods and legendary heroes of a particular people.

N

Natchez Trace — an important trail or route between Nashville, Tennessee, and Natchez, Mississippi, used by frontiersmen on their return journey after floating their products downriver to market in New Orleans.

National Road — an important pioneer road extending from Cumberland, Maryland, to Vandalia, Illinois.

navigable — deep enough and wide enough to afford passage to ships.

O

Ohio River Valley — the great valley that drains into the Ohio River, a branch of the Mississippi River.

Ohio Territory — that part of the great Northwest Territory which was admitted to the United States as the state of Ohio, March 1, 1803.

Old Kaintuck — early nickname for Kentucky.

overseer — superintendent, supervisor.

P

packet boat — a boat that carries mail, passengers and goods regularly on a fixed route, usually along a river or the coast.

pallbearer — a person who helps to carry the coffin at a funeral.

pallets — a small, hard, or temporary bed often on the floor.

pillion — a pad or cushion put on behind a man's saddle chiefly for a woman to ride on.

pirogues or canoes — a dugout or a boat like a canoe.

Promontory — the place in Utah where the first transcontinental railroad in America was completed on May 10, 1869, when California's Governor Stanford drove in the final spike, made of gold.

prospector — person who explores an area for mineral deposits.

puncheon bench — bench made from split log or slab with face or top smoothed and legs attached.

puncheon floor — floor made from split logs or slabs with the faces or tops smoothed.

Q

quirt — riding whip with a short handle and a rawhide lash.

R

railheads — the end of a railroad line.

rawhide seats — seats made from untanned cattle skins.

recollections — the action or power of recalling to mind.

redeem — to buy back, to get or win back.

Revolutionary War (1775-1783) — the war in which thirteen British colonies won their freedom and became the independent United States of America.

rough-hewn — formed crudely without smoothing or finishing.

rural — of or relating to the country, country people or life, or agriculture.

S

sadiron — a flat-iron pointed at both ends and having a removable handle.

saltpeter — potassium nitrate or sodium nitrate.

salt spring — a source of salt water issuing from the ground.

sausage stuffers — a device for stuffing a highly seasoned minced meat in casings of prepared animal intestine.

saw mill — a mill or machine for sawing logs.

schottische — a round dance in double measure similar to the polka, but slower.

serape — a woolen blanket worn by Spanish-American men as a cloak or poncho.

Seward Peninsula — a peninsula in Alaska named for William Henry Seward, the man who arranged for the purchase of Alaska from Russia.

sheared — cut or clipped wool from sheep.

slate pencils — pencils of material that is visible on slate.

slates — a tablet of slate used for writing on.

slivers — untwisted strands of textile fibers produced by a carding or combing machine or tool and ready for spinning.

snuff — a preparation of pulverized tobacco to be inhaled through the nostrils.

Society for the Prevention of Cruelty to Animals — the name for many groups of people who work to prevent mistreatment of animals.

sod — grass-covered surface of the ground.

sourdough — 1. a veteran inhabitant and especially an old-time prospector of Alaska or Northwestern Canada; 2. fermented dough saved from one baking to start fermentation in the next, such as was used by the original prospectors in the Yukon.

spectacles — any of various things felt to resemble a pair of glasses.

spiles — spouts inserted in maple trees to draw off sap.

sugaring — to form sugar by cooking or boiling the sap of maple trees.

supernatural — of or relating to an order of existence beyond the visible observable universe.

surveyor — one that practices the art of surveying land.

Swedenborg, Emanuel — a Swedish scientist, inventor and mystical religious leader who lived from 1688 to 1772.

T

tableau — a static depiction of a scene usually presented on a stage by costumed participants.

tallow dips — candles made by dipping string or wick into tallow and repeating until crude candles were formed.

tall tales — exaggerated stories.

tambe — little drum-like instrument.

tanner — one who converts hides into leather by treatment with an infusion of tannin-rich bark.

tatting — a delicate, handmade lace formed usually by looping and knotting with a single cotton thread and a small shuttle.

tavern — an inn where alcoholic beverages are served.

terrapin — any of the various edible North American turtles living in fresh or brackish water.

tiller or wide-bladed oar — a lever used to turn the rudder of a boat from side to side.

Toby Tyler — a story written by James Otis in which the experiences of young Toby, a boy who ran away from his uncle to spend ten weeks working for a circus, are described.

tomcod — any of several small fishes resembling the related common codfish.

traction — the adhesive friction of a wheel on a rail as it moves.

transcontinental — extending or going across a continent.

treadle — a lever device pressed by the foot to drive a machine.

trek — an organized migration by a group of settlers.

turnpike — 1. a revolving frame bearing spikes and serving as a barrier or gate (toll bar); 2. a toll road or one formerly maintained as such.

V

Varsouvienne — a popular pioneer dance done to three-quarter time music.

vise — any of various tools having two jaws for holding work that closes usually by a screw or lever.

voyageur — a man employed by a fur company to transport goods and men to and from remote stations in the Northwest usually by traveling in canoes.

W

wanderlust — strong or unconquerable longing for or an impulse toward wandering or moving about.

War of 1812 — A war in which the United States sided with France against England in a struggle for freedom of the seas.

Warrior's Path — the Indian path followed by Daniel Boone in blazing the Wilderness Trail through the Cumberland Mountains.

Wilderness Trail or Road — an important pioneer trail blazed by Daniel Boone and leading from Virginia through the Cumberland Gap into central Kentucky.

wood ash lye — lye made by pouring water through ashes of wood.

wooding — loading wood or fuel aboard steamboats.